Reclaiming Thecla

An Introduction to the
Acts of Thecla

Reclaiming Thecla

An Introduction to the
Acts of Thecla

Vincent Skemp and Gina Christ

Claremont Press
Claremont, CA

Copyright © 2022 Claremont Press

Reclaiming Thecla: an introduction to the Acts of Thecla / by Vincent Skemp and Gina Christ
    xii + 192 pp. 22 x 15 cm.
    ISBN 978-1-946230-59-1 (paperback)
    ISBN 978-1-946230-61-4 (ebook)

First printing, 2022

Cover art: Fresco of Saint Thecla in Savior-Transfiguration Cathedral, Chernihiv, Ukraine. Public domain photograph obtained via Wikimedia Commons.

Claremont Press
www.claremontpress.com
1325 N. College Ave
Claremont, CA 91711

Contents

Preface

Our work on the *Acts of Thecla* began in the Master of Theology program at St. Catherine University in St. Paul, Minnesota. The *Acts of Thecla* was part of Vincent Skemp's New Testament survey course in 2009, which led to Gina Christ writing a master's thesis with Skemp as advisor. Christ's thesis, *The Thecla Narrative: Gender, Eschatology, and God's Patronage in Second Century Social-Sexual Identity* (2013), focused on engaging the text's social and theological messages around gender and was chosen for the Abigail Quigley McCarthy Center for Women's Research and Creative Work Award. Simultaneously with the thesis, Skemp led a Greek reading group on the *Acts of Thecla* and Xenophon of Ephesus's *An Ephesian Tale*, which was also part of Christ's introduction to Koine Greek. The thesis and reading group proved to be the beginning of years of work and reading toward what has become this introduction to the *Acts of Thecla*.

While waiting for the most recent critical edition of the *Acts of Thecla* and seeking to assist students, Skemp undertook translations of the *Acts of Thecla*, both from the Greek Richard A. Lipsius edition and the French translation of the forthcoming critical edition by Willy Rordorf, et al. (Appendix 1). Revised forms of those translations are now part of this introductory volume. While reading the Greek, we continually amended the Lipsius edition and paid particular attention to the language of self-control and modesty in comparison with similar language in Greek literature, especially in Paul's letters and the Greek romances. Since the authors of the forthcoming Greek edition, here translated from French in Appendix 1, had access to many more manuscripts than were available to Lipsius, readers should consult Appendix 1. At times, we will discuss important differences between these translations.

When we teach small groups or classrooms, the questions surrounding the Thecla text typically have very little to do with how the *Acts of Thecla* relates to the Christian canon and more to do with the text itself: Where has this text been? Was it intentionally buried, à la *The Davinci Code*? So, while our interest was academic and focused on grounding the text in its original context, when we have introduced the *Acts of Thecla*, the primary questions from students often concern why they had never heard of it before. We took these sorts of questions as a clue that an introductory book about the *Acts of Thecla* would be helpful.

The *Acts of Thecla*, the story of a woman who cast off social expectations, traveled alone, and taught in the ancient world, strikes many as amazing when first reading it. The centrality of her story of perseverance and agency is strikingly different from the caricature of the obedient and silent women who often occupy peripheral locations in the Gospels. Thecla's life is in danger throughout the narrative, especially from her own mother and Alexander. While Thecla's strength and resilience makes students wonder if the *Acts of Thecla* is a proto-feminist story, a deeper examination reveals complications with that sort of reading.

We wrote this introduction to the Thecla narrative in Minnesota on the ancestral homelands of the Dakh'ota People in the midst of the COVID-19 pandemic, which disproportionately affects BIPOC communities. As educators of European descent and therefore settlers,[1] we believe we must learn from indigenous peoples and that we have an obligation to honor and respect the first people and recognize their caring for our common home. Other sovereign American Indian nations, including the Anishinaabe, also have a long history with these sacred lands, past, present, and future. We endeavor to deepen our awareness of our complicity in the complex history of colonialism, genocide, and broken treaties. This short statement is an effort to acknowledge our complicity and is but a small step toward deepening our understanding of our participation

---

[1] For the term settler and other related terms, see Byrd, *The Transit of Empire: Indigenous Critiques of Colonialism*; Morgensen, "White Settlers and Indigenous Solidarity."

in interlocking systems of oppression. We embrace an anti-racist mode of interpretation that includes commitment to the journey of working toward dismantling these systems. We encourage readers to learn about native-led initiatives to address a host of matters, including voluntary land taxes at the Native Governance Center website and the restorative justice land recovery website Makoce Ikikcupi.[2]

Our approach to the Thecla story is textual and dialogical, that is, we read the text in conversation with other interpreters. While we focus predominantly on the voices and roles of women in the text and the struggles women likely faced in that ancient context, the Greco-Roman world, we believe that the *Acts of Thecla* can still speak to us today if we are willing to think deeply and creatively. Acknowledging the importance of intersectionality, our exploration of the Thecla narrative embraces a feminism that aims to be anti-racist. Inspired by womanist theologian Raquel St. Clair's "hermeneutics of wholeness," we seek the wholeness of everyone without aiding or abetting oppression.[3] We will at times draw analogies to our present contexts as a way of engaging an actualization of the text for us today, including drawing connections to people who challenge the evil of systemic racism, both past and present. As we were concluding this introduction to the Thecla story in Minneapolis in 2020–2021, in addition to the COVID-19 pandemic, George Floyd was murdered two miles from our respective homes. The subsequent civil rights movement against police brutality and the unrest and trial were at the forefront of our minds as we composed this introduction.

Insofar as Thecla is simultaneously embedded in traditional cultural systems and values of the Greco-Roman world, the character frequently presses the original audience to rethink how those systems and values need not exclude the vision put forward in the narrative. An analogue for today is the Queer Tango Project.[4]

---

[2] https://nativegov.org; https://makoceikikcupi.com.

[3] St. Clair, "Womanist Biblical Interpretation," 59–60.

[4] For information about the Queer Tango Project and resources, see https://queertangobook.org.

Based on a traditional form of dance that heretofore had been restricted to carefully defined gender roles, the Queer Tango Project is entirely rooted in a traditional dance form and seeks to reimagine it in a less exclusive way. Just as dancing is a form of expression that is open to everybody, we believe that the *Acts of Thecla* is a story about a form of Christian spirituality that is available to all. Written in a time when Christianity was fractured and uncertain, Thecla's story reminds us that participation is unlimited.

Acknowledgements

We are grateful to many people who have assisted our work on this project over the past few years, including our families, especially Deirdre, Rafa, and Esme. The Confraternity of Christian Doctrine with the Catholic Biblical Association of America provided Skemp with a generous sabbatical grant to promote Catholic biblical literacy and interpretation. In agreement with that grant, we use the New American Bible (NAB) when quoting biblical passages other than our own translations. We also received two Research and Scholarly Activities grants through St. Catherine University in 2016 and 2020. We are also grateful for the support that the St. Catherine University Theology Department provided when we presented our research on the *Acts of Thecla* in the "Thinking Theologically" series, April 14, 2016.

We wish to take a moment to express our gratitude to several indigenous people who are instrumental in our learning and teaching: Jim Bear Jacobs and Bob Klanderud for the Sacred Sites tour, which teaches about areas in the Twin Cities sacred to indigenous people, and Ramona Kitto Stately and Ethan Neerdaels for the Bdote workshop through the MN Humanities Center. While the tour and workshop are a small part of their work, those events are life-changing.

Finally, we express our gratitude to Tom Phillips for working with us when we began the process of publishing this volume through Claremont Press and to James Rogers and Andrew Schwartz for seeing it through to completion.

Chapter 1

Introduction and Translation

We are so excited to introduce the *Acts of Thecla* (*ATh*) to you. We decided to write this book after studying the *ATh* for several years. Scholars who write about the *ATh* often focus on how Thecla relates to Paul, the other main character of the story, and women in the early church as well as what the story can tell us about gender in Greco-Roman culture. We will introduce you to some of those discussions in this book, give you our perspectives, and invite you into the conversation. It is our goal to present many different perspectives and interpretations of this engaging text. We are hoping to add depth to your experience by explaining the social context, pointing out a possible rhetorical strategy, and connecting the text to other Christian writings and traditions. We are not trying to identify and advance one correct method of interpretation. Rather, we hope to assist your understanding and add some color to an ancient text, bringing it to life. It may seem at times that we are giving contradictory explanations, and it is possible that we are. Our goal is to invite voices into a lively discussion and bring new voices to it as well.

The Thecla narrative is rather short: forty-three paragraphs. In this chapter we summarize the story, introduce the characters, and conclude with a translation of the narrative. Please consult that translation when we refer to the story and its characters by paragraph number (1–43).

Chapter 2 offers an overview of the connections between the *ATh* and Greek romances. The *ATh* follows the pattern of these wildly popular romances in which lovers have an initial meeting,

1

separate, undergo various trials and adventures, and then typically reunite in a happy ending. The romances not only help illuminate patterns in the story, but also the stated purpose of the romance genre explains why the author of the *ATh* chose to emulate that genre even though the romance focus on erotic love created certain difficulties. The Greek romances enable us to answer questions about aspects of the text that may seem unusual or unique.

Chapter 3 introduces the concept of patron-client relationships in the Greco-Roman world. Like capitalism today, this is a social system that is not easily defined but ran through daily life as an organizing concept. And just as capitalism drives us to think about relationships in terms of transactions, patron-client relationships were not just a means of moving goods and services through social layers; they were also a way of understanding hierarchical relationships. We introduce the concept of patron-client relationships because it affects how ancient audiences likely would have understood the relationships between all of the characters in the narrative, including God as patron and protector.

Chapter 4 compares the points of tension and agreement between the *ATh* and the Pastoral Epistles. There are names, locations, and themes that connect these texts, each offering its own appropriation of the Pauline tradition and the theological question of salvation. Exploring multiple points of view in theological discourse, ancient and modern, including the various tensions in the first two centuries of the Christ movement, deepens our engagement with the *ATh*.

Chapter 5 consists of a series of questions and responses about selected aspects of the *ATh* that often arise. These responses are part of larger conversations and may be useful for adding to your understanding of aspects of the *ATh* not touched on in the other chapters of this book. In addition to socio-historical, narrative, and theological matters, the Q&R chapter addresses two particularly thorny questions: How might we appropriate the *ATh* responsibly today? Is the *ATh* a feminist work?

Brief Summary of the *Acts of Thecla*

The *A Th* is a second-century Christian narrative that follows the transformation and journey of Thecla of Iconium, whose life is upended when she hears Paul preach. The *A Th* is part of a larger work, the *Acts of Paul* (AP), comprising chapters 3–4 of that work. The first chapter of the *A Th*, which consists of the first twenty-five paragraphs and a little of paragraph 26, takes place in Iconium, Thecla's hometown. Iconium was in Asia Minor, which is now Turkey. The second chapter, paragraphs 26–43, is in Antioch, where Thecla faces a second set of trials. There were two cities called Antioch in antiquity, Pisidian Antioch and Syrian Antioch, and the narrative does not completely resolve the ambiguity.[1] The chapters only loosely relate to each other rhetorically, leading some to conclude that they were likely two different stories knitted into one with a single leading character. There are themes that are consistent through both chapters (paragraphs 1–25 and 26–43), but only Paul and Thecla are present in both until the end, where there is an effort to tie up the story.

As the narrative opens, we meet Paul entering the city of Iconium. The story thus begins in medias res with Paul in "flight," which lends an ominous tone (like scary music in horror movies), suggesting a possible martyrdom to early listeners. However, divine intervention saves Thecla in the end! In this first part of the narrative, Thecla comes into the picture after Paul is welcomed into a house church, seated and teaching. Adherents of Jesus, now called Christians, typically met in homes, sometimes crowded tenement dwellings. Thecla, however, comes from a wealthy home that is without a male head of house. Thecla is the girl next door who can only hear Paul teaching through her window but cannot see him. Paul's words profoundly affect her, and she falls silent for three days. This silence disturbs Thecla's mother, who calls Thamyris, the man betrothed to Thecla, to the scene. It becomes clear that Thecla is

---

[1] The matter is complicated by the variant readings in the Greek manuscripts and other versions of the *A Th*. Rather than try to resolve the problem, we direct readers to commentaries such as Pervo (*Acts of Paul*, 151–52) for an account of the issues involved in the debate.

reconsidering her betrothal because of what she hears Paul teach. When Paul is thrown into prison, Thecla bribes her way into the prison to learn more about "the word of God" from him. The two are discovered together; Paul is expelled from Iconium, while Thecla is sentenced to burn in the town square at her mother's suggestion. Thanks, Mom! Thecla is miraculously saved from the burning with rain and an earthquake, reunites with Paul outside the city, and the two head off to Antioch together.

Just outside the Antioch city gates, a powerful citizen named Alexander approaches Paul and Thecla. Alexander accosts Thecla but is rebuffed, which sets the two against each other. Paul disappears from the story at this point. Alexander wants Thecla tossed into the arena and killed for rejecting and shaming him in public, including removing his imperial garments, which is a sacrilegious violation of Roman symbols. There is a trial. Thecla is sentenced to die in the arena. At the trial, an elite woman named Tryphaena with familial connections to Caesar takes Thecla into her home until it is time for Thecla's martyrdom. Tryphaena thereby protects Thecla from losing her purity (chastity) through rape while in prison. Thecla's sincerity impresses Tryphaena. In the arena, a variety of animals miraculously protect Thecla, there are fantastic natural occurrences (special effects!), such as lightning, the women of the city cry and throw herbs, and Tryphaena faints — all playing a role in saving Thecla from death. Thecla prays and baptizes herself in a pool of water filled with dangerous animals. It becomes obvious to the governor that Thecla is protected by a significant power. The games are stopped, Thecla proclaims her allegiance to "the living God," and she is set free.

In the final paragraphs of the narrative (40–43), Thecla sets off to find Paul in a place called Myra. She locates him, tells him about what happened in Antioch, and Paul bids her to go and continue to teach "the word of God." Thecla heads back to Iconium to testify to her faith, asking her mother if she can come to believe the message she offers. Thecla's testimony to her mother is that her adherence to Christ offers a different kind of wealth. Her final words to her mother, that if she wants children, then "look, here I am!" would almost certainly have been viewed by a Greco-Roman audience as extremely odd. In that culture, there was nothing more important than for a matron to provide children for posterity, to carry on the family honor and traditions. In the final sentence, Thecla is placed in the town of Seleucia, where she is established as a teacher, eventually dying a natural death.

Original Language and Date of Composition

The *Acts of Thecla* was composed sometime in the mid- to late-second-century CE, originally in Greek. The African church father Tertullian refers to it around 198–203 in his treatise on baptism (*De baptismo* 17.4–5), which marks the latest time it could have been composed. Most scholars think that oral forms of the story circulated prior to its composition. The *A Th* was translated into several other languages, including Coptic, Syriac, Armenian, and Latin. The original Greek versions of the story are not entirely uniform, and sometimes the story as it appears in these other languages may contain an earlier version than the one found in the Greek forms. There may even be parts of the narrative that derive from early oral tradition. Speculations abound! As time passed from its first compositions in the second century, the story underwent further additions. The fifth-century Greek *Life and Miracles of Thecla* paraphrases the second-century Greek work, with strategic additions (particularly miracles) and omissions that amount to one of the earliest commentaries on the second-century work.[2] The Thecla story was popular for centuries after it was first composed and was well known throughout the Middle Ages. Thecla was considered a saint in the Catholic Church until Vatican II (early 1960s), and she is still a saint in the Eastern Orthodox Church.[3]

---

[2] The fifth-century *Life of Thecla* is available in Dagron, *Vie et Miracles de sainte Thècle: Texte grec, traduction et commentaire*. See Johnson, *The Life and Miracles of Thekla: A Literary Study*; Honey, *Thekla: Text and Context with a First English Translation*.

[3] Regarding these matters, see Rordorf, "Tradition and Composition in the Acts of Thecla"; Pervo, *The Acts of Paul*.

Apocryphal Acts of the Apostles

The *Acts of Thecla* is categorized together with a group of second-century extra-canonical Christian writings called the Apocryphal Acts of the Apostles (AAA). As the name suggests, apostles are the leading characters of these stories: the Acts of Peter, John, Andrew (with and without Matthew), Thomas, and Paul, among others. Each of the stories within the AAA gives us a snapshot of beliefs within a particular community. The AAA are often compared and contrasted with the canonical Acts of the Apostles because they expand on the saga of missionizing for individual apostles, usually starting with a post-resurrection mission that concludes with martyrdom. In the AAA there is a greater focus on chastity, including within marriage, and women play an even larger role in the spreading of the early movement's message. Scholars look to these works for evidence of women's roles and diversity of ideas among the growing communities. They provide a picture of early house churches, second-century Christian teachings, and social struggles within the early movement.

The *Acts of Paul* is one of several extracanonical texts about apostles. Scholars think that the *A Th* originally circulated independently and then was at some point inserted into the *AP*. A hint that the two works were originally separate is that the *AP* refers to the holy Spirit several times, whereas the *A Th* never mentions the holy Spirit. This omission is interesting because the late second century was a time in which some Christians were recoiling from a seeming overemphasis on the holy Spirit among a group called Montanists. We discuss this matter further in chapter 5.

Here is an image to illustrate the *AP* and the *A Th* among the AAA:

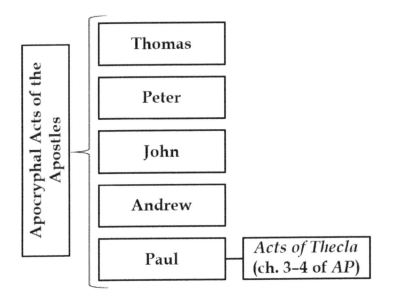

In many ways, the *AP* and the *ATh* within it embody typical features of the AAA. For further exploration of these fascinating texts, see the introductions available, including Klauck, *The Apocryphal Acts of the Apostles: An Introduction.*

The Canonical Pauls and the Paul of the *Acts of Paul and Thecla*

The importance of Paul to Christian history cannot be overstated. For many people, Paul is second in importance only to Jesus. This level of influence and deep history are part of what make Paul complicated and significant.

The canonical texts of the New Testament contain at least three Pauls: the author of the genuine letters that the apostle Paul wrote (which are not without internal tensions), Luke's depiction of Paul in the Acts of the Apostles, and the Paul of the disputed letters written in his name. Even the latter, which many scholars doubt go back to Paul himself, are not uniform. Outside of the canon, we have the way Paul is depicted in the second-century *AP* and also the way Paul is depicted in the *ATh*. There is thus some tension even between the Paul of the *AP* and the Paul of the *ATh*.

The historical Paul wrote letters in the 50s and early 60s; he therefore lived perhaps one hundred years before both the *AP* and the Thecla narrative were written. The Paul in the Acts of the

7

Apostles is a character developed by an author, Luke, probably in the late first century, which is several decades later than Paul's genuine letters. The relationship of Luke's Paul to Paul's genuine letters is debated and need not detain us here other than to assert that for historical points about the apostle Paul scholars tend to look primarily to his genuine letters. For introductions to Paul's letters in the New Testament in relation to the Acts of the Apostles, see Soards, *The Apostle Paul: An Introduction to His Writings and Teachings*, 7–13; Phillips, *Paul, His Letters, and Acts*, 5–49.

The Apocryphal Acts, however, are useful in giving us a window into how Paul was being appropriated by different factions in the early communities. There was not a universal understanding of Paul's teachings, even within one hundred years of the historical Paul's existence. These divergent views of Paul and his teachings imply that second-century Christians disagreed about who Paul was, who best carried on his legacy, and which of his teachings were of primary importance. The *A Th* is often read in light of the second-century conflict about the legacy of Paul regarding changes in emphasis on marriage and family given the delay of the return of Christ.[4] The following grid may assist you in visualizing the various Pauls in the first two centuries:

---

[4] MacDonald, *Legend and the Apostle*, 97–103.

The Paul in the undisputed letters	• Actual letters Paul wrote in the 50s CE: 1 Thessalonians Romans, 1–2 Corinthians, Galatians, Philippians, Philemon • Paul identifies as a Hebrew born of Hebrews, an Israelite
The Paul in Acts of the Apostles	• After the Gospel, Luke's second narrative was composed in the late first century • Paul is a hero of the nascent Jesus movement, which Luke calls "The Way" • Paul spreads the Word of Christ and performs miracles
The Paul in the Pastoral Epistles	• Second-century appropriation of Paul's authority in letter format: 1–2 Timothy and Titus • Unknown author(s), often designated as "the Pastor," writing in Paul's name
The Paul in other disputed letters	• Ephesians, Colossians, 2 Thessalonians. Author(s) and dates disputed.
The Paul in the *Acts of Paul*	• Extracanonical second-century narrative expansion of Acts of the Apostles
The Paul in the *Acts of Thecla*	• Extracanonical late second-century narrative insertion into the *Acts of Paul*

The Importance of the *ATh*: Women in the Christ Movement

Tertullian's information about the *ATh* reveals that a woman named Quintilla was using Thecla as a model to follow regarding baptism. Through Tertullian's criticism of women baptizing and teaching, we learn that women were doing such activities. (Tertullian invoked 1 Cor 14:33–35 as forbidding women to teach and baptize.) Women teaching in the early centuries of the Christian movement is affirmed in Paul's genuine letters and in Acts 18:26 but stands in tension with the Pastor's perspective in 1 Timothy 2:12 (cf. 1 Cor 14:34–36) regarding women teaching men. In presenting Thecla as engaging in public ministry, this story stands in the tradition of female apostleship — Thecla is much like Junia (Rom 16:7) — and in tension with the growing tendency to curtail women's roles found, for example, in 1 Timothy and Tertullian. Although Thecla begins the narrative silent (7–10), as the story progresses she

9

teaches the governor (37–38), and by the story's conclusion Paul authorizes her to teach (40) and she "enlightened many with the word of God" (43). When she bluntly informs Paul that she has been baptized (40: "I received the washing"), her actions affirm the blessing Paul states in his beatitudes (6: "blessed are those who observe baptism"). Tertullian's negative reactions to Quintilla's use of the *A Th* illustrates tensions among Christians regarding women's roles in the late second century.

Although the *A Th* has many fictional aspects, Carolyn Osiek and Margaret MacDonald remind modern readers that we should not lose sight of the fact that the story is "a symbolic depiction of what was at stake especially for women who joined the church and worked to secure its survival and expansion in various ways."[5] They rightly note that the story of Thecla displays "a combination of women's initiative, social expectations concerning women's proper roles, and the special significance attached to honorable behavior of women in defining group identity."[6] The *A Th* is a text that leads to important discussions on gender dynamics and women's roles in the Christ movement of the second century.

Characters and Their Significance
Thecla

Whether Thecla existed historically is unclear but also unlikely. Fruitful engagement with the *A Th* as a story need not address the question of Thecla as an historical figure. It is our position that biblical and extracanonical stories need not be historically verifiable to be meaningful, a topic we return to in chapter 5.

The *A Th* describes Thecla as a young female from a leading family in the city of Iconium. She may have been in her early teens, although her precise age is not indicated.[7] Presumably her father is dead, as he is never mentioned. That there is no male head of household is strikingly similar to Jesus in Mark's and John's Gospels. Thecla is betrothed to an elite man named Thamyris. Her life of

---

[5] Osiek and MacDonald, *A Woman's Place*, 242.

[6] Osiek and MacDonald, *A Woman's Place*, 241.

[7] See Horn, "Suffering Children, Parental Authority," 121–30.

10

privilege is set out for her: She will continue to be wealthy, continue to own slaves, and will become a powerful matron of a leading family, just as her mother hopes and expects. Things do not work out quite so expectedly, however, after she hears Paul's message from the safe confines of the family home, listening to him from a window. As J. D. McLarty notes, when we first encounter Thecla in the story (7), "Thecla's description as 'betrothed' puts her on the threshold of a change in status, just as she is physically situated at a liminal position of the house, at the window."[8] Paul's message about "self-control and resurrection" (6) changes her life and sets her on a course away from the safe and comfortable expectations of her mother. That Thecla comes to this new faith through hearing Paul is reminiscent of Rom 10:17: "Faith comes from what is heard" (NAB).

After hearing Paul's message, Thecla falls silent for three days. This silence can be interpreted as recognition that the new spirituality she is incorporating is so overwhelming that she cannot speak. Or perhaps the silence indicates implicitly that Thecla is at a crossroads and facing a period of indecision as she ruminates on the possibility of a new, unforeseen path that has suddenly complicated her life's trajectory. In addition, the silence may hint at a forthcoming defiance against the social expectations being imposed on her by her mother and the larger culture. In the narrative, had Thecla married Thamyris as planned, she would have become an honored matron raising children, continuing a life of wealth and privilege. Abandoning that elite trajectory on account of her hearing Paul is *the* linchpin of the plot.

She sneaks out of her house (18) to visit Paul in prison, bribing the prison guard with expensive items, one of the many indications of her elite social location in the narrative. When Paul and Thecla are caught together, they are brought before civil authorities, Paul is thrown out of the city, and Thecla is sentenced to burn at the stake at the urging of her mother (20).

Thecla is saved by a miracle involving an earthquake and rain; she is either thrown out of the city or voluntarily leaves to seek Paul.

---

[8] McLarty, *Thecla's Devotion*, 169–70.

11

She finds Paul, asks to follow him, and even offers to cut her hair (25). Paul declines her offer, as he is worried about the trials that lie ahead for her. She asks to be baptized. It seems, at this point in the story, that Thecla believes baptism confers some sort of special protection, that she will be safe if baptized. Paul tells her to be patient.

At the beginning of the Antioch segment (26), an elite man named Alexander attempts to acquire Thecla as they are entering the city, first by asking for Paul's permission, and then through force. Thecla's beauty makes her vulnerable to Alexander's desire. Intriguingly, Paul does nothing to help her, refusing to assume the role of Thecla's patron. Thecla fights back with such ferocity that she made Alexander "a laughing stock." For publicly shaming him, Alexander drags Thecla before the governor, which sets forth Thecla's next trial.[9]

An elite woman, Tryphaena, takes Thecla into her home until she faces death in the arena. Doing so preserves Thecla's chastity. The next morning, Thecla is taken to the arena. After surviving many trials, the governor asks Thecla who she is, and she responds by testifying to her faith.

The *ATh* closes with Thecla seeking Paul a final time. She finds him, tells her story, and receives his blessing to teach. Upon returning to Iconium, she testifies to her mother, prays in the spot where she first had heard Paul teaching, and dies a natural death later. In contrast with martyr narratives but congruent with the Greek romances, there is a happy ending. The final line mentions Seleucia, a location where the historical basilica of Thecla stood.

Paul

The first paragraph of the text introduces Paul as he enters Iconium, where he is greeted by Onesiphoros, Paul's host. Paul's

---

[9] The encounters with Alexander occur in two of the four key events in the narrative that take place in a liminal space, which is a permeable space between boundaries, often home (*oikos*) or city (*polis*): (1) Paul entering Iconium, (2) Thecla at the window, (3) Thecla and Paul approaching Antioch, and (4) Alexander at Tryphaena's door to take Thecla to her death.

primary role in the *A Th* is as evangelist and teacher who mediates God's message, the word of God concerning self-control and resurrection (see Box 1 below regarding self-control). In contrast to the *AP*, Paul in the *A Th* is not a miracle worker. The *A Th* is in essence the story of Thecla's response to Paul's offer of salvation that she hears from her window when Paul teaches a series of blessings in 5–6 that signal to the audience the beliefs held dear to whomever composed this apocryphal work.

A particularly interesting aspect of the depiction of Paul in the *A Th* is that Paul seems unaware of potential dangers at times. He does not detect Demas and Hermogenes as liars (1), when even Onesiphoros alerts Paul that they are hypocrites (4). Paul is portrayed humorously in the tomb when reunited with Thecla (23), where he is surprised to see her because he was only just praying for her safety. A crucial moment occurs outside of the gates of Antioch when Paul denies any connection to Thecla (26), thereby exposing her to danger. After that incident, he disappears from the story until Thecla once again seeks him out and finds him to tell her story. It may seem strange to people today reading the *A Th* for the first time that it might depict Paul in ways that are not entirely flattering.

However, the *A Th* largely depicts Paul positively, as an authoritative teacher. In addition to the blessings that begin the narrative, Paul has a strong and supportive following throughout. Moreover, Paul is likened to Christ during Thecla's first persecution (21): When she is about to be burned, she sees "the Lord sitting as Paul," which may be an allusion to Romans 8:29 ("For those he foreknew he also predestined to be conformed to the image of his Son, so that he might be the firstborn among many brothers"). Paul's role as mediator of the message of salvation makes this comparison to Christ, the mediator of salvation, more intelligible. Paul's authority is demonstrated for a final time near the end of the story when he authorizes Thecla to go forth as an apostolic mediator and teacher. Thecla follows directly in Paul's footsteps.

Box 1: The Importance of Self-Control

The Greco-Roman world placed great emphasis on self-control and self-mastery; therefore, it is no surprise when the narrator introduces Paul's beatitudes as "the word of God concerning self-control" (5). One beatitude is "blessed are the self-controlled." One of the sayings at the oracle of Delphi, in addition to the more famous "know thyself," is "nothing too much" or "nothing in excess," an encapsulation of the "golden mean" regarding moderation.

The historical Paul also thought that self-mastery of the body was important, a point that relates to his preference for celibacy and begrudging allowance for marriage (1 Cor 7). For Paul, the primary solution to the problem of the body's passions and desires is the holy Spirit (Gal 5:22–24; cf. 1 Cor 9:24–27). Paul does not go the route of positing a body-soul dualism in which the immortal soul is imprisoned in the mortal and corruptible body. One of the more interesting points about the *ATh* is that for all of its focus on a "wayward world" (17) and the need to renounce the world and maintain bodily purity and chastity (5), it depicts Thecla as lacking self-control at times, which we examine further in chapter 2 on the Greek romances. Also significant, the *ATh* does not avail itself of the key way of addressing the problem of the body's passions and desires that we find in Paul's letters: The *ATh* never mentions the holy Spirit. Paul in his seven genuine letters and Paul in the *ATh* converge in the need to transcend this world through self-mastery.

Further reading: Stowers, "Paul and Self-Mastery"; Johnson, *Among the Gentiles*, ch. 6.

Other Characters in Iconium
Demas and Hermogenes

The first line of the narrative introduces us to Demas and Hermogenes and identifies them entirely negatively as "full of hypocrisy." They join Paul as travel companions on the way to

14

Iconium, and as such the *ATh* begins with internal tension among Christians: Paul is walking into the city with people who present themselves differently from how they are so that the audience can anticipate that they will cause trouble in some way. Particularly condemnatory in a text in which love language plays such an important role, the narrator says that Demas and Hermogenes flatter Paul "as though they love him." The verb for love in that sentence is agapic love. The narrator notes that Paul loved them nonetheless paternally, employing a different Greek verb typically used for the love of parents for children. We further examine the importance of love language in chapter 2 and return to it again in the conclusion.

The choice of the names Demas and Hermogenes is not accidental, as they are derived from 2 Timothy, a matter we explore in chapter 4.

These two characters try to get Paul killed by giving Thamyris the idea that he should denounce Paul as a Christian (14), an element of the plot that mirrors actual second century situations regarding denunciation of Christians found in governor Pliny the Younger's letter to Emperor Trajan (composed ca. 110–112 CE). Following their advice, Thamyris calls Paul in front of the governor to stop him from teaching that young people should not marry but rather remain virgins. They also misrepresent Paul's teachings. They offer to teach Thamyris about an understanding of resurrection that is contrary to Paul's message. Demas and Hermogenes are presented as insincere and not following the tenets of the faith that Paul teaches.

Onesiphoros

The next character we meet is Onesiphoros, whose residence is next door to Thecla's mother's house. He is connected to Paul through Titus, providing yet another connection to the Pastoral Epistles. Onesiphoros hosts Paul in Iconium. The narrative presents him as the model Christian "family man" by naming his children and wife (2), which implies how important children are to Christians despite the fact that Thecla has chosen celibacy. Onesiphoros takes in Demas and Hermogenes at Paul's request, even though he can discern that they are not genuine Christians (4: "I do not see in you fruit of righteousness").

At the end of the Iconium portion of the story, Onesiphoros has left everything and followed Paul, which implies that he has taken on an ascetic life with his entire family, although it is not clear that he and his wife have embraced chastity, which is often an element in other Apocryphal Acts. He has chosen to leave "the things of the world" (23) in conformity to Paul's teaching (6: "Blessed are those who depart from the appearance of the world"). The tomb location symbolizes Onesiphoros's radical ascetic life. In apparent approval of Onesiphoros's choice, the narrator comments that "in the tomb there was much agapic love" and happiness (25). The scene clearly invokes a eucharistic celebration: "They had five loaves and vegetables and water [and salt] and they rejoiced over the holy deeds of Christ." With this character we have another connection to the Pastoral Epistles, as 2 Timothy 1:16 and 4:19 refer very positively to Onesiphoros (1:16: "He often gave me new heart and was not ashamed of my chains") and his family. Onesiphoros models a way of being an ascetic Christian different from Thecla's celibate witness and Tryphaena's witness as a wealthy widow.

Theocleia and Thamyris

Theocleia is Thecla's mother and Thamyris is the man that Thecla is to marry. The two of them are deeply tied to the elite Iconian social order. Since Thecla has no father, her mother and her betrothed would have been the two people who determined her future. Until Paul arrives, they are the most powerful people in Thecla's life. They are flummoxed by Thecla's sudden silence and do not understand her new faith, nor do they want to. The honor and social position of Theocleia's household would be completely upended if Thecla does not marry Thamyris as planned. Thamyris can certainly reject a woman, but rejection by a woman endangers his social position.

After Thecla falls silent for two days, Theocleia calls for Thamyris to persuade her back to her proper place. These two characters' actions are driven by the honor-shame social system of the Greco-Roman world (see Box 2 below). Theocleia insists that her

16

daughter be burned alive (20) rather than suffer the shame of Thecla's refusal to marry. Thamyris yells at Thecla, "Turn back to your Thamyris and have shame!" (10). Thamyris's primary role is that of the jilted lover obsessed with marrying Thecla, unconcerned that she no longer wants to and frightened of the strange passion that has taken hold of her. There are many such jilted lovers in the Greek romances. Both Theocleia and Thamyris misconstrue her passion as a sexual desire for Paul.

Box 2: Honor-Shame in the Greco-Roman World

People in the Greco-Roman world were enmeshed in a system of honor and shame that was graded in a hierarchy of gender and social privilege with wealthy, elite male citizens at the top and enslaved noncitizens at the bottom. Honor-shame was a core public value in the Roman Empire. Honor is a claim to social value that is publicly acknowledged. The wealthy are born with honor, prestige, inherent social value. Shame, in general, is its opposite, although there are two types of shame. To "be shamed" is to have no honor or to be diminished in public honor. To "have shame," paradoxically, is positive, as it means that the person knows the importance of honor and place. To "have shame" is closely associated with modesty and the regulation of female behavior. When Thamyris tells Thecla to "turn back to your Thamyris and have shame!" (10), he is invoking the positive sense of shame — that she should return to accepting the publicly recognized place of honor and privilege that she is throwing away if she does not return to their betrothal. Negative shame is on display in section 26 when Thecla humiliates Alexander publicly. He has "been shamed" (27) because she stripped him of his honor and worth in the eyes of others. Alexander treated Thecla as though she were a slave without any claim to or concern for family honor. It is difficult for people in the twenty-first century from individualistic cultures to grasp the importance of honor-shame values in group-oriented (dyadic) cultures; these values dominated

> public and private life and social expectations in ways
> unfamiliar to those steeped in cultures that value individualism.
>
> See Plevnik, "Honor/Shame"; Osiek and MacDonald, *A
> Woman's Place*, 7–9 and ch. 5.

It is Thamyris who gathers a crowd and brings Paul before the governor using the initial charge of false teachings. Once the courtroom scene starts, Thamyris drops out of the story entirely. At the end of the story, Thecla returns to Iconium to have one final conversation with her mother, Theocleia, and finds out that Thamyris is dead.

Governor Castillius

In the Iconium segment the provincial governor is named and mentioned in connection with two trials of Paul and Thecla (14–15, 21). The text does not have an entirely negative depiction of the governor. The narrator lets the audience know that the governor enjoyed listening to Paul talk about the holy deeds of Christ (20). After Theocleia insists that Thecla be executed, the text includes an ambiguous statement about the governor's emotions. The narrative can be read as saying that the governor "was greatly moved" — possibly by the mother's words — or that he "suffered greatly" — possibly out of reluctance to determine the sentence. Whatever the governor's precise emotions, he sentences Paul to be scourged and expelled from the city and Thecla to be burned per her mother's wishes. The effort to depict the governing authorities as somewhat sympathetic to the Jesus movement becomes even more pronounced with the governor in the Antioch segment and follows in the footsteps of the Acts of the Apostles in tempering the depiction of Gentile authorities in somewhat positive ways.

Antioch Characters

Alexander

We meet Alexander outside the city gates of Antioch (26). He is described in some of the Thecla manuscripts as "head of the provincial council" but in others as simply "Syrian." The provincial council had powerful civic responsibilities directing the local imperial cult. When Alexander sees Thecla, he immediately desires her (26). Since she is with Paul, Alexander logically thinks that Thecla is Paul's wife, concubine, or slave; he therefore seeks to acquire Thecla through Paul by means of wealth and gifts. When Paul states truthfully that he has no claim on Thecla, the effect is that Alexander assumes that she must be an enslaved prostitute and grabs at her. In the process of defending herself, she removes Alexander's imperial regalia (26), causing him public shame and dishonoring the sacred symbols of his imperial authority. We discuss this incident in more detail in the chapter on patronage. For now we note that Thecla's attack on Alexander's garments would be understood in that culture as hostility toward imperial authority, an authority that is aligned with the imperial cult, and it stands in contrast to the more favorable depictions of the governors in the *ATh.*

For a different perspective on imperial authority in the *ATh* in relation to the *AP*, see Pervo, *The Acts of Paul*, 150. Regarding the Roman imperial cult, see Price, *Rituals and Power: The Roman Imperial Cult in Asia Minor.*

Some versions of the *ATh* indicate that Alexander was patron and judge of the "games" (27), which were a variety of spectacles for public entertainment. After the initial trial, Alexander arrives at Tryphaena's home to bring Thecla to the arena. Tryphaena first turns Alexander away, and he must return with soldiers to forcibly get Thecla. During the time that Thecla is in the arena, Alexander continually tries to introduce different beasts and new ways to kill her. Despite the miracles that prevent her execution, Alexander remains committed to killing Thecla in an effort to regain his honor. Margaret MacDonald explains, "By defending herself with strength and courage, Thecla has assumed the traditional role of the male in the public honour context. Alexander feels bound to answer the challenge in an equal or more forceful way" (*Early Christian Women and Pagan Opinion*, 176). It is Alexander who asks the governor to end the games after Tryphaena faints.

Tryphaena and Falconilla

Tryphaena is described as an elite woman of Antioch who is related to the emperor (36). The text refers to her as "queen" twice (27 and 36), which does not mean she was royalty; rather, "queen" was an honorific title given to female patrons.[10] Tryphaena crucially takes Thecla into her home between the time of her trial and going to the arena, which preserves Thecla's chastity; Thecla otherwise would have been vulnerable to sexual assault in prison.

Tryphaena claims that her dead daughter, Falconilla, implored her in a dream to shelter Thecla so Thecla in turn could pray for her so that she would go to "the place of the righteous" (28). We are not told how Falconilla died. Tyrphaena's response to that dream sets in motion her surrogate motherhood and patronage of Thecla. She names Thecla heir to her wealth (39) and through Thecla supports Paul's ministry financially (41). Tryphaena is convinced of Thecla's sincerity and the power of her connection with God and defends her strongly when Alexander comes to take her away. When Thecla is in the arena, Tryphaena saves her by fainting, causing everyone to think that she has died. Her fainting frightens Alexander out of his determination to kill Thecla, prompting him to beg the governor to end the games.

Tryphaena stands in sharp contrast to characters in the story who treat Thecla out of concern for public perception. Thecla's mother, Theocleia, is willing to sacrifice her daughter to maintain her social status and family honor, and Alexander tries to execute Thecla to rectify his having been shamed and to restore his honor. By contrast, Tryphaena uses her social status to protect Thecla.

The Governor in Antioch

Unlike Governor Castillius in Iconium, the governor in the Antioch segment is unnamed. The depiction of Gentile authorities positively continues with this unnamed governor, as the text depicts him as weeping when Thecla throws herself into the water (34)

---

10 Hylen, *A Modest Apostle*, 83.

"because the seals were going to eat such beauty," and he becomes exceedingly sad (35) when Alexander suggests that they tie Thecla to two bulls. The governor's response, "Do what you want," deflects the responsibility to some extent from himself onto Alexander. When Tryphaena faints and people think she has died, the governor's reaction is unclear. The text states that he "was taken aback," but it could also be translated that he "had had enough." Either way, the governor orders a halt to the proceedings. He then calls Thecla forward to explain herself and her miraculous protection, asking a series of questions. Thecla's testimony is her first public teaching.

With the increasingly positive depictions of the governors, the *ATh* relates to other Christian texts that display an interest in portraying governing authorities as to some extent positively disposed to the Jesus movement (Acts 25:25–27; 26:30–32). Early Jesus movement groups had varying degrees of willingness to accommodate aspects of the surrounding culture.[11]

The Women of Antioch

A group of women of Antioch appear seven times in the Antioch portion of the *ATh*, demonstratively commenting on the action taking place, taking part in the action at one point; throughout the trial and persecution of Thecla, they provide a collective dissenting voice. These women behave in ways similar to a chorus insofar as they are the conscience of the narrative and are a significant rhetorical device that guides the audience to view the events from their perspective, in support of Thecla. On the second occasion, the women are with their children (28), which signals to the audience that they are respectable mothers. These women embody the audience response to Thecla's ordeals.[12]

When Thecla is condemned to the animal arena, the women cry out, "Wicked judgement! Impious judgment!" (27) In reaction to the charge of sacrilege, the women and children yell, "Oh god! An

---

[11] For further exploration of that matter, see Carter, *The Roman Empire and the New Testament*, 14–26; Pilgrim, *Uneasy Neighbors*.

[12] McLarty, *Thecla's Devotion*, 189.

impious judgment is occurring in this city!" (28). The women present a counterargument to the people clamoring for Thecla to be brought out (32) when they yell back, "May the city be uprooted for this injustice! Take all of us, proconsul! Bitter spectacle! Evil judgment!" These women are seen shouting, grieving (33), weeping (34), and ululating (35), a high-pitched indication of mourning, a ritual still present in many cultures to this day. Some of the women take action in defense of Thecla by throwing herbs (35), which causes the animals to become sleepy and thereby not harm her. Allusions to a chorus in 4 Maccabees, a martyr text, further illustrate that the author likely intended this collective group of women to have a role similar to a chorus. In addition to echoing a chorus, portrayals of groups of women who respond to the events unfolding in the Greek romances *Callirhoe*, *Daphnis and Chloe*, and *An Ephesian Tale* are another important influence. For these parallels, see chapter 2.

The *Acts of Thecla*
A Translation

The following translation by Vincent Skemp is based on the Richard Lipsius edition.[1] See also Appendix 1 for a translation of the forthcoming critical Greek edition.

1 When Paul was going up to Iconium after the flight from Antioch, traveling companions were with him, Demas and Hermogenes the metal worker; being full of hypocrisy, they earnestly beseeched Paul as though they loved him agapically. Paul, however, looking only at the goodness of Christ, did nothing bad to them but loved them paternally very much so that he sweetly told them precisely all the sayings of the Lord [and teachings and exposition of the Gospel concerning] the birth[2] and resurrection of the Beloved as well as the mighty acts of Christ—as it was revealed to him.

2 And when a certain man named Onesiphoros heard that Paul had arrived in Iconium, he entered with his children Simmias and Zenō and his wife, Lectra, into the presence of Paul so that he might receive him. For Titus had described Paul to him. For he had not seen him in flesh but only in spirit.

3 And he proceeded on the king's highway toward Lystra and stationed himself eagerly awaiting him, watching those coming based on Titus's information. He saw Paul coming, a small man in

---

[1] Lipsius and Bonnet, *Acta apostolorum apocrypha*, 1:235–72.

[2] Lipsius's text in this sentence presents particular difficulties. See Appendix 1 (pp. 141–54), which is based on many more Greek manuscripts than were available to Lipsius.

size, bald in the head, curved in his legs, healthy, with a unibrow, with somewhat of a long nose, full of goodwill. For sometimes he appeared like a man; at other times he had the face of an angel.

4 Upon seeing him, Paul smiled at Onesiphoros. And Onesiphoros said, "Greetings, servant of the blessed God."

And he responded, "Grace be with you and your house."

Demas and Hermogenes were jealous, and they were aroused to greater hypocrisy so that Demas said, "Are we not of the Blessed One, that you do not greet us in this way?"

And Onesiphoros said, "I do not see in you the fruit of righteousness. If you are persons of importance, rest here in my house."

5 And when Paul entered into Onesiphoros's house, there was great joy and bending of knees and breaking bread and the word of God concerning self-control and resurrection, with Paul saying:

Blessed are the pure in heart,
for they will see God.

Blessed are those who keep the flesh undefiled,
for they will become temples of God.

Blessed are the self-controlled,
for God will speak to them.

Blessed are those who renounce this world,
for they will please God.

Blessed are those who have wives as though they did not,
for they will become God's heirs.

Blessed are those who have fear of God,
for they will become angels of God.

6 Blessed are those who are in awe of the sayings of God,
for they will be consoled.

Blessed are those who receive the wisdom of Jesus Christ,
for they will be called children of the Most High.

Blessed are those who observe baptism,
for they will rest with the Father and the Son.

Blessed are those who possess the insight of Jesus Christ,
for they will be in light.

Blessed are those who depart from the appearance of the world
for the sake of the love of God,
for they will judge angels and they will be blessed at the right of
the Father.

Blessed are the merciful,
for they will be shown mercy and they will not see the harsh Day
of Judgment.

Blessed are the bodies of virgins, for they [their bodies] will
please God and they will not lose the reward of their purity,
for the word of the Father will become for them saving action on
the day of his Son and they will have rest forever and ever.

7 And as Paul was saying these things in the midst of the community
in the house of Onesiphoros, a certain Thecla, a virgin, whose mother
was Theocleia, betrothed to a man named Thamyris, was sitting near
the window of the house, listening night and day to the message
about purity spoken by Paul. And she did not move from the
window, but she advanced in faith with abundant joy. Yet also [as]
she watched many women and girls go in to [hear] Paul, she also
longed to be considered worthy to stand before Paul and to listen to
the word of Christ. For she had not yet seen Paul's distinctive
features but had only heard the message.

8 As she would not leave the window, her mother sent for Thamyris.
He came very gladly, as he already was taking her in marriage. Then
Thamyris said to Theocleia, "Where is my Thecla?"

And Theocleia said, "I have a new tale to tell you, Thamyris: For
three days and three nights Thecla does not rise from the window,
neither to eat nor to drink, but gazes intently as if enraptured, as
devoted to the man, a stranger, who teaches with beguiling and

crafty words, so that I am astonished at how this young woman's sense of modesty is so grievously troubled.

9 "Thamyris, this man is inciting the city of Iconium, as well as your Thecla! All the women and young people go in to him and are taught by him that it is necessary, he says, to show reverence to the one and only God and to live chastely. And still my daughter, like a spider at the window imprisoned by his words, is controlled by a new lust and a gravely powerful passion. For she observes closely the words spoken by him, and the young woman is conquered. But you go to her and speak. For to you she is betrothed."

10 And as Thamyris was approaching, since he both loved her and feared her disturbed passion, he said, "Thecla, my betrothed, why are you sitting like this? And what passion has stupefied you? Turn back toward your Thamyris and have shame!"

And still her mother kept saying these things: "Child, why do you sit looking below so and answer with nothing but madness?"

And they wept bitterly, Thamyris for his woman gone astray, Theocleia for her child, and the female slaves for their mistress. There was much commotion in the grief-stricken house. While these things were happening, Thecla would not be turned away but kept observing closely the word of Paul.

11 Thamyris, however, sprang up, went into the street, and he watched closely those going in to Paul and those coming out. And he saw two men fighting among themselves bitterly. And he said to them, "Men, who are you? Tell me. And who is the one inside with you leading astray young minds and deceiving maidens so that they don't get married but should remain as they are? I promise to give you many things if you tell me about him. For I am first of the city."

12 And Demas and Hermogenes said to him, "Who this man is, we do not know. But he would deprive young men of wives and young women of husbands, saying, 'In particular, there is no resurrection for you if you do not remain pure and do not pollute the flesh, but keep pure.'"

13 Thamyris said to them, "Come, men, into my house and rest with me." And they went into a very costly banquet with much wine and great wealth and splendid table. And Thamyris plied them with drink out of his love for Thecla and desire to obtain her as his wife. And Thamyris said at the feast, "Men, tell me. What is his teaching, so that I might know? For I am in terrible agony about Thecla, that she loves the stranger and I will be deprived of marriage."

14 Then Demas and Hermogenes said, "Bring him to Governor Castellius for inciting the crowd with the new teachings of the Christians, and so he will destroy him and you will have Thecla as your wife. And we will teach you that what he calls resurrection has already happened when we have children [and that we are raised when we come to know the true God.]"

15 Thamyris, hearing these things from them, and full of jealousy and rage, arose at dawn, went to the home of Onesiphoros with magistrates and public officials and a considerable mob with clubs, and said to Paul, "You corrupted the city of Iconium and the one betrothed to me, so that she does not want me. Let us go to Governor Castellius."

And the entire mob said, "Take away the magician! He corrupted all of our women!" And the mob agreed.

16 And standing before the (tribunal) platform, Thamyris said with a loud cry, "Proconsul, this man, we do not know from where he comes, who does not allow maidens to be married. Let him say before you why he teaches these things."

Demas and Hermogenes said to Thamyris, "Call him a Christian and in this way you will destroy him."

The governor stood firm in his intention and called Paul, saying to him, "Who are you and what do you teach? For they denounce you in no small measure."

17 And Paul lifted up his voice, saying, "If I am being examined today for what I teach, listen, proconsul: A living God, a God of vengeance, a jealous God, a God in need of nothing who desires the salvation of human beings, sent me so that I might draw them away from destruction and (moral) impurity and every pleasure and death, so that they no longer sin. Therefore, God sent his Son, whom I preach and teach that humanity has hope in Him who alone has shown compassion for a wayward world, so that humans are no longer subject to judgment but have faith and fear of God and knowledge of dignified behavior and love of truth. Therefore, if I teach the things revealed to me by God, what do I do wrong, proconsul?" When the governor heard this, he ordered that Paul be bound and led away into prison until there might be an opportunity for a more thorough hearing.

18 At night, Thecla removed her bracelets, gave them to the doorkeeper, and when the door had been opened for her, she entered into the prison. She then gave a silver mirror to the prison guard, went in to Paul, and sitting at his feet, listened to the mighty deeds of God. And Paul felt no fear, but in the bold confidence of God, he held sway. And with her faith growing, she kept kissing his chains.

19 Meanwhile, Thecla was being sought by her own (people) and Thamyris. Since she was missing, they looked for her in the streets, and some of the fellow slaves of the prison guard disclosed that she had gone out at night. They interrogated the prison guard, and he told them that she had gone to the stranger in the prison. They went as he told them and they found her acting in the manner of someone imprisoned by familial love. After leaving there, they drew together the crowds and appraised the governor.

20 And he ordered that Paul be brought to the tribunal. But Thecla rolled around at the spot where Paul had taught while sitting in prison. So, the governor ordered that she be brought to the tribunal. And with joy she departed rejoicing.

When the crowd drew near again to Paul, they more fervently shouted, "He's a magician! Take him away!"

The governor liked to listen to Paul about the holy deeds of Christ. And after having a consultation, he called Thecla, saying, "Why do you not marry Thamyris according to Iconian law?" But she kept standing, looking intently at Paul.

As a verdict was not yet determined, Theocleia, her mother, cried out, saying, "Burn the lawless one! Burn in the midst of the amphitheater the one who refuses to be a bride, so that all the women who have been taught by this man may become fearful."

21 The governor was greatly moved. After having Paul scourged, he cast him outside the city, and he sentenced Thecla to be burned. Immediately, the governor got up and went to the amphitheater. The entire crowd also departed for the violence of the spectacle. But Thecla was like a lamb in the desert looking around for the shepherd, so she sought Paul. And looking into the crowd, she saw the Lord sitting like Paul and said, "As (if) I am unable to endure, Paul came to watch over me." And she paid close attention to him, focusing intently. But he went away into heaven.

22 The young boys and maidens brought firewood and grass to burn Thecla. When she was brought in, naked, the governor wept and he was amazed at the power in her. They spread out the firewood, and the executioners ordered her to mount the pyre. While making the mark of the cross, she mounted the wood. They then set it on fire. Although the fire glowed tremendously, the fire did not touch her. For God, having compassion, made a subterranean noise and a cloud above full of water and hail overshadowed [them], and the entire vault (of heaven) poured forth so that many also were in danger of dying; thus the fire was extinguished and Thecla saved.

23 Paul was fasting with Onesiphoros and his wife and children in an unsealed tomb on the road they were traveling on from Iconium to Daphne. When many days had passed during their fast, the children said to Paul, "We are hungry." But there was nothing to buy bread with, for Onesiphoros had left the things of the world and followed Paul with his whole household.

Paul took off his outer garment and said, "Be gone, child. Buy more bread and bring [it back]."

While the boy was shopping, he saw Thecla, the neighbor. And he was startled, and said, "Thecla! Where are you going?"

Then she said, "I've been looking for Paul ever since I was saved from the fire." And the boy said, "Come with me. I will bring you to him. For he sighs deeply for you, praying and fasting for six days already."

24 When she came upon the tomb, Paul was kneeling and praying, and saying, "Father of Christ, do not let the fire touch Thecla, but be with her, for she is yours."

Standing behind (him), she shouted, "Father, you made the heaven and the earth, the Father of the beloved Son, Jesus Christ, I praise you, for you saved me from the fire so that I may see Paul."

And standing up, Paul saw her and said, "O God, knower of hearts, the Father of our Lord Jesus Christ, I will praise you because what I had asked for you have done quickly for me, and you listened to me."

25 And there was inside, in the tomb, much agapic love while Paul, Onesiphoros, and everyone rejoiced. They had five loaves and vegetables and water [and salt] and they rejoiced over the holy deeds of Christ.

And Thecla said to Paul, "I will cut my hair, and I will follow you wherever you may go."

But he said, "The present age is shameful and you are beautiful. [I fear that] another trial will overtake you, worse than the first, and you may not endure [it] but behave cowardly."

When Thecla replied, "Only give me the seal in Christ and a trial will not touch me," Paul said, "Thecla, be patient and you will receive the water."

26 And Paul sent Onesiphoros with his entire household back to Iconium. And so, taking Thecla, he went to Antioch. As they were jointly entering, a certain Alexander, head of the provincial council, upon seeing Thecla, desired her intensely, and he entreated Paul earnestly with wealth and gifts.

But Paul said, "I do not know the woman of whom you speak. Nor is she mine." With considerable strength, he embraced her in the street.

She, however, would not put up with it but sought Paul and cried out bitterly, saying, "Do not violate the stranger! Do not violate the slave of God! I am first among the Iconians, and it is because I do not wish to be married to Thamyris that I am thrown out of the city." And grabbing hold of Alexander, she tore off his mantel, took away the crown from his head, and made him into a laughingstock.

27 Feeling both attracted to her and at the same time having been shamed by what happened to him, he led her to the governor. When she admitted that she had done these things, he condemned her to the animals. [Alexander organized the animal games.] And the women were astonished and cried out to the tribunal, "Wicked judgment! Impious judgment!" Thecla then asked the governor that [her] purity remain until she fights with the wild beasts. And a certain wealthy [queen] named Tryphaena, whose daughter had died, took her into her safekeeping and had her for a consolation.

28 When the animals were led in procession, they bound her to a fierce lioness, and Queen Tryphaena kept following behind her. The lioness upon which Thecla was sitting, however, licked her feet, and the entire crowd was shocked. The charge inscribed was "sacrilegious person."

The women with the children cried out from above saying, "O god! An impious judgment is occurring in this city!"

And after the procession Tryphaena took her in again. For her daughter Falconilla, who had died, said to her in a dream, "Mother, you will take the stranger, the undefended Thecla, in my place so that she may pray for me and I may be transferred into the place of the righteous."

29 When Tryphaena took her in after the procession, she felt grief both because she was going to fight the beasts the next day and also she loved her [vehemently like her] daughter Falconilla. She said, "My second child, Thecla. Come pray for my child so that she may live forever, for I saw her while sleeping."

Without delaying, she lifted her voice and said, "My God, the Son of the Most High, who is in heaven, grant to her according to her wish so that her daughter Falconilla will live forever." And when Thecla had said these things, Tryphaena grieved, realizing that such beauty was to be thrown to the beasts.

30 And when dawn arrived, Alexander came to fetch her, for he produced the beast hunts, saying, "The governor is seated and the crowd clamors for us. Hand (her) over (that) I may convey her to fight the beasts."

Tryphaena cried out to flee from him, saying, "A second grief of my Falconilla has come upon the house, and no one is helping, neither a child, for she has died, nor a kinsman, for I am a widow. O God of Thecla, my child: Help Thecla!"

31 And the governor sent soldiers so that Thecla would be brought forth. Tryphaena, however, would not stand down, but taking her hand, she escorted her, saying, "I conveyed my daughter Falconilla to the tomb; you, O Thecla, I will convey to fight the beasts."

And Thecla wept bitterly and groaned to the Lord, saying, "O Lord God, in whom I believe, to whom I fled seeking refuge, who delivered me from the fire, grant a reward to Tryphaena, who has shown compassion to your slave because she kept me chaste."

32 Tumult ensued with the clamor of beasts and the shouting of the people and the women seated together, with the former saying, "Bring in the one who has done sacrilege!" with the latter saying, "May the city be uprooted for this injustice! Take us all, proconsul! Bitter spectacle! Evil judgment!"

33 Then Thecla, taken from the hands of Tryphaena, was stripped, and she received a sash and was thrown into the amphitheater. As the lions and bears were thrown against her, a fierce lioness, running toward her, laid down at her feet, and the crowd of women shouted out greatly. Then a bear ran at her; the lioness, however, ran out to meet it and tore apart the bear. Once again, a lion, having been trained by human beings who were under Alexander, rushed at her; the lioness locked together with the lion and (both) were completely destroyed. Then the women grieved more intensely when the lioness who had come to her aid also died.

34 Then they threw in many beasts. She then arose, stretching out her hands in prayer. When she finished the prayer, she turned and saw a great pit full of water, and said, "Now is the appointed time that I be washed." And she threw herself in, saying, "In the name of Jesus Christ on this last day, I baptize myself."

Upon seeing this, the women and the entire crowd wept, saying, "Don't throw yourself into the water!" resulting in the governor weeping because the seals were going to eat such beauty. She then threw herself into the water in the name of Jesus Christ. The seals, upon seeing the flash of fiery lightening, floated dead. There was around her a cloud of fire so that neither the beasts touched her nor was her nakedness seen.

35 The women, however, when other more fearful beasts were thrown in, began ululating, and some threw herbs: some nard, others cassia, others cardamom, so that there was a mass of fragrances. Then all the beasts slackened, as if overcome by sleep, (and) did not touch her. At that point, Alexander said to the governor, "I have exceedingly fearful bulls. Let us tie the beast fighter to them!"

And becoming glum, the governor issued an order saying, "Do what you want." They bound her by the feet between bulls and put red-hot irons under their genitals so that, agitating them greatly, they might kill her. They then, therefore, were leaping about. The scorching flames burned through the ropes, and it was as if she was not bound.

36 Tryphaena fainted standing alongside the arena upon the sideboard so that the female slaves said, "Queen Tryphaena is dead!" And the governor was taken aback, and the entire city was frightened.

And Alexander, falling to the feet of the governor, said, "Have mercy on me and the city and release the beast-fighter woman. Do not let the city be destroyed! For if Caesar hears this, quickly he will destroy us and the city, since his kin, Tryphaena, died near the sideboard."

37 The governor then called Thecla from the midst of the beasts and said to her, "Who are you? And what divine beings are with you that none of the beasts touched you?"

Then she said, "I am slave of the living God, who is with me. I believe in his Son, in whom God is well pleased, on account of whom not one of the beasts touched me. For he alone is the pillar of salvation and foundation of eternal life. For he is refuge for those tossed by the storm, relief for those in tribulation, protection for those who are in despair. In sum, whoever does not believe in him will not live but will die forever."

38 The governor, having heard these things, ordered that clothing be brought, and said, "Put on the clothes."

She then said, "The one who clothes my nakedness among the beasts, he will clothe me with salvation on the Day of Judgment." And taking the clothes, she put them on.

Immediately, the governor issued a decree, saying, "I release to you Thecla, the slave of God, the God-fearing one."

All the women cried out with a great voice, and as from one mouth they gave praise to God, saying, "There is one God who saves Thecla!" so that the entire city was shaken by the voice.
39 Tryphaena also came upon the good news with the crowd, embraced Thecla, and said, "Now I believe that the dead are raised.

Now I believe that my child lives. Come inside and I will put in writing [that] all my property is for you." Thecla went with her and rested in her home for eight days, teaching her the word of God, with the result that most of the female slaves also came to believe, and there was a great joy in the home.

40 Thecla kept longing for Paul and kept searching for him, sending out messengers everywhere. It was reported to her that he was in Myra. Taking some young male and female slaves, girding herself and making the garment into a coat in a male style, she went into Myra and found Paul speaking the word of God. As she approached him, he was amazed to see her and the crowd that was with her, wondering if some additional trial was not at hand for her. When she became aware of this, she said to him, "I received the washing (of baptism), Paul. For the one who works with you for the good news has also worked with me for my washing."

41 And taking her hand, Paul led her into the house of Hermias. He listened to everything from her, so that Paul was greatly amazed, and those listening were strengthened and prayed for Tryphaena. And rising up, Thecla said to Paul, "I am going to Iconium."

Paul then said, "Go and teach the word of God." Tryphaena sent her much clothing and gold so that she might set these aside for Paul for the ministry to the poor.

42 She went to Iconium, entered the house of Onesiphoros, fell to the ground where Paul used to sit teaching the sayings of God, and she wept, saying, "O my God, and the God of this house where the Light illuminated me. O Christ Jesus, the Son of God, my helper when I was in prison, helper in the presence of governors, helper in the fire, helper against the beasts. You indeed are God. And to you is the glory forever and ever, Amen."

43 She found Thamyris dead, although the mother was still alive. Summoning her mother, she said to her, "Theocleia, mother, can you come to believe that a Lord lives in heaven? For if you long for wealth, a Lord[3] will give it to you through me. If (you long for) a child, look, here I am!" After testifying in this way, she went to Seleucia, and after having enlightened many with the word of God, she fell asleep with a good sleep.

---

[3] There is no definite article in the Greek of the Lipsius edition. See the translation in Appendix 1 for the likely original reading: "God will give them [riches] to you."

Chapter 2

The *Acts of Thecla* and Greek Romances

This chapter introduces how vitally important the Greek romances were to the composition of the *ATh*. We first provide a brief overview of the Greek romance genre in general, the major aspects of shared plot elements and the purpose of the genre, and then compare and contrast those stories with the *ATh*. Examining the purpose of the romance genre helps to explain why the *ATh* found that genre fit for imitating in important ways. The *ATh* reconfigures the genre for its own purposes; particularly important is the way the *ATh* reshapes the language of love from romantic-erotic love to familial and agapic types of love while maintaining a strong debt to the emphasis on desire in relation to the virtues of purity, self-control, and endurance in the romances.

What are the Greek Romances?

Five Greek "love and adventure" novels have survived almost completely intact from Greco-Roman antiquity: *Callirhoe*, *Daphnis and Chloe*, *An Ephesian Tale*, *Leucippe and Clitophon*, and *Ethiopian Tales*. There is a set pattern to these stories:

- A young man and young woman from elite families, known for their beauty, purity (female), modesty (female), and self-control (male), fall in love at first sight.
- The lovers swear fidelity to each other but must endure separation and many trials away from home; these trials threaten their ability to remain faithful and chaste.

- After many adventures, which include shipwreck, pirates, deceptions, and enslavement, the lovers are ultimately reunited in a return home.

There are variations on this set pattern because these novels have their own characters and often have their own complicated and convoluted plots. However, the basic pattern of the romances above occur in the *ATh*, as do many of the same leitmotifs, such as the importance of revelatory dreams, the mistaken assumption that a hero or heroine has died, and concern for endurance and maintenance of chastity in the midst of trial, to name just a few. There are of course important differences between the romances and the *ATh*. To take one example, the ending of a story tells the reader a great deal about the story. The romance genre strives to have a happy ending with closure (cf. *Call* 8.1), wherein the couple is finally united in a return home, where they live happily ever after. The *ATh* shares certain elements of the typical romance resolution of the plot trajectory in the ending, but it also ends differently precisely because marriage is not the primary focus of the story. For the *ATh*, the trajectory of the story leads to a final statement about Thecla's itinerant teaching of both men and women: "She went to Seleucia, and after having enlightened many with the word of God, she fell asleep with a good sleep." Prior to that final statement, Thecla had only taught women (39). In an important sense, then, the *ATh* provides closure. We find out that Thecla imitates her teacher Paul as an itinerant evangelist. The ending ties together some loose strings from the plot: Thymaris has died and Thecla returns home to meet with her mother in Iconium. But in contrast to the return home of the romances, the *ATh* culminates with leaving home.

To get a feel for these stories, we recommend that you read them for yourself, especially *An Ephesian Tale*, *Callirhoe*, and *Daphnis and Chloe*. These tales are available in translation: Morales, ed., *Greek Fiction: Callirhoe, Daphnis and Chloe, Letters of Chion*; Trzaskoma, trans., *Two Novels from Ancient Greece: Callirhoe and An Ephesian Story*; Reardon, ed., *The Collected Ancient Greek Novels*. On the Greek romance as a genre, see Reardon's *The Form of Greek Romance*. Whitmarsh's *Dirty Love* queries the genre designation and seeks to reorient the Greek romances as part of a much larger corpus.

Some of these Greek romances were composed before or near the era in which the *ATh* was likely written. Our focus is on the *ATh* in relation to *Callirhoe* (*Call*), *Daphnis and Chloe* (*DC*), and *An Ephesian Tale* (*ET*) because *ATh* 20 borrowed directly from *ET* 2.7–8, but there are also strong links to *Call* and *DC*. It is highly likely that the author was familiar with some form of those three stories. We will occasionally note parallels with *Leucippe and Clitophon*, although that novel is distinct in its use of the first person and deviates from the typical ending.[1] *Ethiopian Tales* is not taken into consideration because it dates to the fourth century.

Purpose of the Romance Genre

The prologue to *Daphnis and Chloe* describes a painting of a love story, stating that the painting contains various adventures that typically occur in "the many wonderful things that make up a romance."[2] The prologue also states what the painting, and implicitly therefore, a romance, "is intended" to do, highlighting the role of consolation and teaching: "to heal the sick and to console the afflicted, bring back memories for those who have known love, and to give instruction to those who have not." The pedagogical intent of romances includes reflections on what love is and on various aspects of virtue, including self-control, moderation, purity, chastity, and the danger of passion.

The purpose of the romance genre, as stated in the prologue of this volume, helps to make sense of the fact that the author of the *ATh* found something about that genre useful for Christian storytelling. The *ATh* reflects on these matters in its own way and in particular offers a sustained narrative exploration of the importance

---

[1] Whitmarsh, *Dirty Love*, 157.

[2] Translations from the Greek are from the following, with Vincent Skemp's ad hoc adjustments based on the Greek: Chariton, *Callirhoe*, in *Greek Fiction: Callirhoe, Daphnis and Chloe, Letters of Chion*, trans. Rosana Omitowoju, 3–134; Longus, *Daphnis and Chloe*, in *Greek Fiction: Callirhoe, Daphnis and Chloe, Letters of Chion*, trans. Phiroze Vasunia, 135–210; Xenophon, *An Ephesian Tale*, in *Collected Ancient Greek Novels*, trans. Graham Anderson, 125–69.

of familial and agapic love, self-control, and maintaining purity vis-à-vis the dangers of passion in characters such as Thamyris and Alexander. Furthermore, the romances are replete with miraculous deliverances of pious heroes in the midst of suffering. The author of the *ATh* was also likely drawn to the ways in which the romances provided space to rethink society's traditional gender roles in which women are subordinate to men and exist mainly to bear children and manage the household.[3] Elite women in the romances navigate male power structures in ways that embody key social norms, such as modesty, while also taking advantage of social norms to achieve results not normally available to women. Lest we miss the obvious, in the Greek romances the heroine is a main character or *the* main character, which makes it a genre particularly fitting for the *ATh*'s focus on a female.

A further consideration regarding the romance genre as assisting to "console the afflicted" is borne out in the stories. A leitmotif of the romances is that characters frequently try to console the hero or heroine (*ET* 5.2, 9, 10; *LC* 3.22; 7.14). Consolation was very important to the *ATh*, as it is one of the beatitudes: "Blessed are those who are in awe of the sayings of God, for they will be consoled" (6). This leitmotif helps explain the allusion to Tryphaena as having Thecla "for a consolation" (27), although precisely who is consoled is not clear. It may refer either to Tryphaena providing solace to Thecla before she was about to enter the arena or to Thecla providing solace to Tryphaena in the impending loss of her second child. These two need not be mutually exclusive.

When Thecla rolls on the ground at the spot where she was with Paul and had heard him teach when he was imprisoned (20), we have a clear parallel with a Greek romance (*ET* 2.7–8). But this incident also creates a problem for the message of self-control in the *ATh* beatitudes (5). Including the incident reveals how central the Greek romances were to the plot of the *ATh*.[4] Clearly, the many positive aspects of the romance genre that attracted the author

---

[3] See Finkelpearl, "Gender in the Ancient Novel."
[4] The Coptic omits Thecla rolling around on the ground.

40

outweighed the problem that Thecla's behavior in this incident may have caused.

Evidence that the *A Th* Was Influenced by the Romance Novels

The following chart demonstrates the clear debt the *A Th* owes to the romances in plot outline and motifs:

Greek Romances	Thecla Narrative
Incomparable **beauty of the hero and heroine** (*ET* 1.1; 2:6–7; *DC* 1.2, 13; *Call* 2.2; 6.7)	Paul has the face of an angel (3); Paul and others acknowledge Thecla's beauty (25; 29; 34)
Elite status of the hero and heroine	References to Thecla's elite status recur (26)
Beauty as bringer of trouble (*Call* 6.6)	Paul connects Thecla's beauty to trials (25)
Love at first sight (*ET* 1.3; *DC* 1.15; *Call* 1.1; 2.3; *LC* 1.4)	The words of Paul put a spell on Thecla (7); Alexander desired Thecla intensely upon seeing her (26)
Lovesickness, sometimes connected to silence, speechlessness (*ET* 1.1, 3, 5, 9; 2.5. *DC* 1.13–14, 17–18, 32; *Call* 1.1; 5.5; 6.3; *LC* 1.6)	Thecla does not eat, drink, sleep or speak (8 and 10).
Connected to improper behavior (Antheia in *ET* 1.3; Manto in *ET* 2.5) Anthia visits her imprisoned husband, rolls at his feet, and clings to his chains (*ET* 2.7–8)	Thecla kisses Paul's prison chains (18) and then returns to roll around on the spot where Paul had taught the mighty deeds of God (20)

Greek Romances	Thecla Narrative
A deception separates the lovers out of jealousy (*Call* 1.4; *DC* 4.7)	Demas and Hermogenes, described as jealous (4), are untruthful to Thamyris about Paul's message (12) and encourage him to bring Paul to the governor for inciting the crowd with his teachings (14).
Travel motif (*ET* 1.10–13; *Call* 1.11–13; *LC* 2.31; 3.9)	Journey to Antioch (25)
Separation (*ET* 2.9; *DC* 2.20; 3.3–4; 4.28; *Call* 1.5–7)	Paul's banishment (21); Paul disappears after Alexander episode (26)
Terrible trials (*ET* 1.13–2.7; 3.8, 12; 4.2; *DC* 1.20–21; 4.12) Leitmotif of accosting the young woman, putting her chastity at risk. Anthia is threatened with rape sixteen times.[5]	Thecla sentenced to death by fire (21); Alexander grabs at Thecla (27); sentenced to death, Thecla fights wild animals in the arena (27)
A rival desires the beautiful young woman and seeks to acquire her through gifts (*DC* 1.15, 18; 3.25; 4.7; *Call* 1.1–2)	Alexander desires Thecla and seeks to acquire her through Paul by means of wealth and gifts (26)
Deliverance through divine intervention (*ET* 2.10–11; 4.2; *DC* 2.25–26, 30; 3.27–28)	Miraculous deliverance in Iconium (22) and Antioch in the arena (34–35) with divine intervention

---

[5] Morales, "The History of Sexuality," 53.

Greek Romances	Thecla Narrative
Benefactors are credited with playing an important role in rescue of a hero (*Call* 1.10; *DC* 4.29)	Tryphaena acts as Thecla's benefactor by taking her into her home (29) to avoid the dangers that prison presents to her purity
Pining for, searching for the beloved (*ET* 2.7, 12, 14; 3.10; 4.4; 5.6, 8; *Call* 7.1; *DC* 4.29)	Paul prays and sighs about Thecla (23); Thecla searches for Paul (23); she "kept longing for Paul and searching for him" (40)
Temporary reuniting (*DC* 2.30; *Call* 5.8; *ET* 1.7)	Temporary reunification in the tomb (24); temporary, final reunification in Myra (40)
Homecoming and giving thanks Happy final, permanent reunification (*ET* 5.13; *Call* 8.1; *DC* 4.29–40) Prayer of gratitude to Isis (*ET* 5.13); prayer of gratitude and inscription to Artemis (*ET* 5.15); prayer of gratitude (*Call* 8.8). Offerings to the nymphs (*DC* 4.37); an altar to Love and a temple to Pan (*DC* 4.39)	Thecla does not have permanent reunification with Paul. She has achieved her goals of baptism and her teaching ministry. Thecla returns to Iconium and testifies to her mother; she offers a thanksgiving prayer in the home of Onesiphoros, the same place where Paul had taught (42)
Heroes are **heirs** to wealth (*DC* 4.24; *ET* 5.6, 9)	Thecla is heir to Tryphaena's "property" (39); Thecla's final words to her mother implicitly address that Thecla will not produce an heir. The story ends with her leaving home as evangelist

Observations on the Connections to the Romances

Let's look more closely at the following leitmotifs, common to the romances, that are also present in the *ATh*: elite status, deception, the use of force that threatens chastity, revelatory dreams, the apparent but mistaken death of a character, and the role of the crowd in support of characters.

All the heroes and heroines of the romance novel are wealthy elites, and the *ATh* follows this pattern. Thecla and Thamyris are born into the most elite families in Iconium. The story of *Daphnis and Chloe* opens with the two raised in a humble bucolic setting, but this element of the romance is so vital that the baby Daphnis is dressed in purple (*DC* 1.2), a royal color, while Chloe has a maiden's belt embroidered with gold (1.5) because they are actually of elite parents. Callirhoe's father is a famous general and the most important man in Syracuse, while Chaereas's father is the second most important (*Call* 1.1). The first line of *ET* describes Lycomedes as "among the most powerful there." Connected to this motif is that the endings of these novels tend to make sure that the heroes return to wealth as heirs after many trials and tribulations (*DC* 4.24; *ET* 5.6; 5.9). Following this trend, *ATh* 39 has Thecla become Tryphaena's heir. Socially elite prejudice toward enslaved people in Greco-Roman culture is evident in a comment Clitophon makes on the scheming slave Sosthenes (*LC* 7.10): It is, he says, typical that when someone of slave status becomes frightened, he is exceedingly cowardly. Although the *ATh* never makes a general comment about enslaved people, the narrative is casual about Thecla owning slaves (10) and taking slaves with her into Myra (40).

A major plot element of the romances occurs in the form of a deliberate deception that separates the lovers out of jealousy. Thus, one of Callirhoe's suitors tells Chaereas a lie about Callirhoe being unfaithful to make him jealous (*Call* 1.4), and suitor Lampis destroys the garden flowers to gain an edge over Daphnis to marry Chloe (*DC* 4.7). This leitmotif finds expression in the *ATh* when Demas and Hermogenes, described as jealous (4), are untruthful to Thamyris about Paul's message (12) and encourage him to bring Paul to the governor for inciting the crowd with Christian teachings (14).

Another common leitmotif in the romances is the attempted use of force on one of the heroes, especially but not limited to the female.[6] This familiar pattern puts the woman's purity and chastity in danger. In this motif, when the woman refuses, the attacker often seeks revenge (*ET* 2.9; 3.11; 5.4; *DC* 1.15; *LC* 6.20-21). For instance, at *ET* 4.5 Antheia uses a sword to kill the man attacking her, for which she is sentenced to die. This recurring motif provides background for when Alexander grabs at Thecla (26). In *Callirhoe*, the use of force is equated with lack of moderation (*Call* 2.7; repeated at 8.7; cf. 6.3), which tells us that Alexander's grabbing at Thecla would likewise have been considered to be a sign of lack of self-control, a lack of moderation.

Mistakenly thinking that someone has died is also a leitmotif in the romances (*ET* 3.7-8; 5.2; *LC* 5.7-8); it is in fact the key turning point in the plot of *Callirhoe* (*Call* 1.4-5) — even though she is only unconscious, everyone thinks Callirhoe is dead and so they bury her in a tomb (cf. *Call* 3.1). Everyone thinking Tryphaena is dead in the *ATh* (36), even though she has only fainted, is indebted to this common motif. The importance of the tomb in *ET* and *Callirhoe*, where the heroine's body is placed (only to be found alive later), may be a partial reason for including the tomb in the *ATh* as the place where the Christians fast, pray, and share a meal (23-25). If the threefold reference to the tomb in the *ATh* in some sense symbolizes Christian renunciation of the world, recalling the beatitude "Blessed are those who depart from the appearance of the world for the sake of the love of God" (6), or if the tomb alludes to Jesus's death and resurrection as linked to baptism (Rom 6:2-4) and eucharist (1 Cor 11:26), the narrator does not make those references explicit.

Divine communication through dreams is another motif very common in romances. In *Daphnis and Chloe*, Chloe's parents dream that the nymphs are handing over Chloe and Daphnis to Love (1.7), and the nymphs tell Daphnis in a dream that Pan will save Chloe (*DC* 2.23). When Chloe's birth father finds out that she is his daughter and was suckled by a ewe, he finally understands his

---

[6] The pirate Corymbus falls in love with Habrocomes (*ET* 1.14), who expresses fear of losing his chastity to the lustful pirate (2.1).

nightly dream in which a sheep makes him a father (*DC* 4.35). Tryphaena's dream in *ATh* 28 shares this common motif: Her daughter Falconilla speaks to her about Thecla, which sets into motion Thecla's mediation of her dead daughter to the place of the righteous.

A final leitmotif concerns the crowds in the *ATh*. Crowds are very active in their reactions to events and Thecla's sufferings. Moreover, the reactions of the crowd in the *ATh* are at times divided along gender lines. This characterization of the crowds and their actions derive from similar crowd reactions in the romances, especially in *DC* and *Call*, less so in *ET* and *LC*.[7] It becomes clear that the crowds assist the audience in navigating the events taking place, which is one of the roles of a chorus.[8] Often we find an indirect allusion to a group having a chorus-like function, as is the case in *ET* 5.4, where the children playing shouted out to Antheia together "at the same time" words that give her hope that she will soon recover her husband. The speaking in unison invokes a chorus.

The primary influence for the crowd reactions in the *ATh* is the depiction of the crowds in *Call* and *DC*. When the crowd of women throw flower petals and herbs in the *ATh* (35), something very similar occurs several times in *Call* (3.2, 8; 8.1). Unique to the *ATh*, however, is that the crowd of women takes action in defense of Thecla by throwing the herbs, which causes the animals to become sleepy and thereby not harm her. Crowd reactions along gender lines recur in *DC* and *Call* (*DC* 4.33; *Call* 5.4; 6.1; 8.7).[9] For instance, in *DC* 4.33 the narrator provides the crowd's reaction of approval, first the men, then the women; the narrator, however, specifies that the women shared in the female's joy, an emotional component not

---

[7] *Leucippe and Clitophon* rarely provides crowd reaction to events. Despite the rarity of crowd reaction in that work, at *LC* 8.14 the entire population gives a loud cry of joy in support of Leucippe and reacts very negatively toward Thersandros, who had challenged Luecippe's chastity.

[8] Sometimes the romance narrative will make an explicit reference to a chorus (*DC* 1.4; 2.29; 4.35; cf. 2.2, which never directly or explicitly links the choral imagery to the crowd).

[9] At *Call* 6.2, the crowd is divided by social status.

said of the men. This sense of solidarity among women is also very strong in the *ATh*.

Throughout the trial and persecution of Thecla in Antioch, a group of women provides a collective dissenting voice. When Thecla is condemned to the animal arena, the women cry out "wicked judgement! Impious judgment!" (27). In reaction to the charge of sacrilege, the women and children yell, "Oh god! An impious judgment is occurring in this city!" (28). Whereas Alexander shows concern for the fate of the city only when Tryphaena appears to have died (36), the group of women in solidarity with Thecla speak in condemnation of the city and its injustice toward Thecla. The women present a counterargument to the people clamoring for Thecla to be brought out when they yell back, "May the city be uprooted for this injustice! Take all of us, proconsul! Bitter spectacle! Evil judgment!" (32). Particularly significant is that these are matrons defending Thecla in public: These women with children represent the intersection of the domestic (*oikos*, the home) and civil (*polis*, the city) spheres for a Greco-Roman audience that associated order in the home as crucial for proper civic functioning and divine favor. These matrons articulate and embody the counterargument to the view that Thecla is a threat to home and city. These women are seen shouting, grieving (33), weeping (34), and ululating (35). The latter is a high-pitched mourning ritual that demonstrates their solidarity with Thecla's suffering.

In sum, the author of the *ATh* was clearly indebted to the romance genre. We have elaborated on six of the many connections the *ATh* shares with the Greek romances: elite status, deception, the use of force that threatens chastity, revelatory dreams, mistaken death, and the role of the crowd. Examining these connections assist in better understanding influences on the composition of the work, rhetorical devices, and key plot points.

Common Elements of the Greek Romances Altered in the *ATh*

Despite these many connections between the *ATh* and the romances, elements central to the romances are absent from the *ATh* or were altered. One such element concerns the importance of the various Greek gods and goddesses. The intervention of the scheming god Eros, Love, who causes disaster to befall the young lovers, is central to the romance plot.[10] The romances refer to erotic love and its accompanying desire in relation to the virtues of self-control and chastity. Thus, in *Call* 2.4 we find that "Eros treats self-control as a personal insult," especially in those who try to be rational about love. Love is a force that has "power over all the gods and even Zeus" (*Call* 6.3). Neither the goddess Fortune nor personified Rumor have roles in the *A Th*. Daphnis and Chloe are said to have been saved by divine providence (*DC* 1.8). Since swearing oaths and taking vows concern calling on the gods to witness—a frequent occurrence in the romances (*ET* 1.11, 16; 2.1, 4; *DC* 2.39; *Call* 2.11; 3.2)—we find no oath taking in the *A Th*. Frequently, the oaths have to do with the preservation of chastity and therefore fidelity to the beloved. For instance, Amphinomus (*ET* 5.2) swears an oath by the sun and the Egyptian gods to preserve Antheia's purity, as does Polyidus (*ET* 5.4). However, just as the god Pan looks after Daphnis and Chloe (*DC* 2.5) and rescues Chloe in miraculous fashion (*DC* 2.25–26), the *A Th* emphasizes that God delivers Thecla.

Although there are no oaths, the *A Th* shows a comparable, deep concern for purity. The beatitudes extol the virtue of purity twice, first at 5 ("Blessed are those who keep the flesh undefiled") and again at 6 ("Blessed are the bodies of virgins, for they will please God and will not lose the reward of their purity"). Thecla asks the governor to guard her purity (27) so that her purity remains until she fights with the wild beasts. Thecla prays (31) that God grant Tryphaena a reward for keeping her chaste, which refers back to the purity beatitude (6). Demas and Hermogenes emphasize Paul's teaching on purity through repetition (12): "There is no resurrection if you do not remain pure and do not pollute the flesh but keep pure."

Another distinct difference: Marriage is a vital part of the romance plot; Thecla, however, refuses to marry after hearing Paul teach. An indication of how vital marriage is to the romance plot is

---

[10] Persecution by a god, central to the Greek romances (a leitmotif derived from the Homeric epic), is absent in the *A Th*.

that in both *ET* and *Callirhoe* the lovers separate and the woman has to marry another man (*ET* 2.13; *Call* 2.11–3.1).[11] Although the *ATh* lacks the marriage motif, characters in the Iconium section of the story misunderstand both Thecla's desire to be with Paul and her silence. They understand her silence as erotic lovesickness when it is actually a desire to take the next steps in her new faith. Thecla's mother thinks Paul is a magician who has cast a spell on her daughter, while Thamyris understands Paul as a rival lover. Thamyris also fears Thecla's "disturbed passion" (10).

Arguably the most significant alteration the *ATh* makes to the romance genre is to transform the language of love from romantic-erotic love to familial and agapic love. Thamyris's love for Thecla (13) and Alexander's desire for her (26 and 27) are erotic love in Greek. Thamyris does not understand that Thecla's love for Paul is a familial love (19), the same sort of love that Tryphaena has for her daughter Falconilla (29). Thecla's desire is not for Paul as lover but as revelatory teacher, and it is Jesus whom the text specifically names as beloved in the very first scene and again in 24. Paul's teachings concern love of truth (17) and the agapic love of God (6): "Blessed are those who depart from the appearance of the world for the sake of the love of God." The narrative specifies the tremendous agapic love in the tomb (25), where they share a meal and rejoice over the holy deeds of Christ. In contrast to Clitophon, who is love's slave (*LC* 1.7 "enslaved to the pleasure of love"), Thecla three times identifies herself as slave of God (26, 31, 37), and the Antioch governor ultimately confirms that identification (38).

The romance stories place enormous emphasis on the beauty of the hero and heroine, and there is an association of goodness with beauty (*ET* 2.11) and badness with ugliness (*ET* 3.12; 5.7). Scholars tend to agree that an aesthetic connotation of the three statements about Thecla's beauty is undeniable.[12] However, the *ATh* is also circumspect about Thecla's beauty. The narrator never describes Thecla's beauty at length, whereas the romances allow the audience

---

[11] McLarty, *Thecla's Devotion*, 48, notes that marriage is the organizing principle of the romantic novels.

[12] Esch-Wermeling, *Thekla-Paulusschülerine wider Willen*, 91.

to gaze at the hero's and heroine's beauty (*DC* 1.13, 24, 32; *ET* 1.1) through descriptions of their bodies. Allusion to the face as in some sense otherworldly or radiant is a shared leitmotif (*Call* 1.1; 2.2; *A Th* 3). Thecla's beauty as "a reason for aesthetic regret at her sufferings"[13] is also a motif of the romance novels. Moreover, Thecla's beauty is connected to prayer, especially in section 29 (cf. 34) in such a way that refocuses beauty from solely the physical to a deeper spiritual element.

Although the *A Th* provides a description of Paul (3), the narrative de-emphasizes Paul's appearance insofar as the story makes it clear that Thecla comes to faith through hearing Paul before she had seen him (7).[14] The *A Th* shares the motif of gazing at the main character, employing similar language to the romances. In *ET* 1.3, the god Eros forces Habrocomes to fall in love with Antheia, and the text states that he stared at her, unable to be released from "the vision." Similarly, in *A Th* 8, Theocleia tells Thamyris that Thecla is fixated on Paul: "She gazed intently as if enraptured." However, the *A Th* inverts this visual aspect of desire in important ways. First, the *A Th* emphasizes the aural aspect—Thecla does not see Paul initially, but only hears him. The word used in the *A Th* repeatedly (8; 9; 10; 20; 21) to describe Thecla's fixation on Paul, often translated as "gazing," has as its basic sense "to observe closely" and can include mental focus.[15] Second, since the information about Thecla gazing derives from Theocleia (8), her way of describing Thecla's fixation on Paul in erotic terms is undermined in the narrative as incorrect when the story refers to agapic and familial love as at the heart of the Christ movement. Significantly, the *A Th* transforms Thecla's gazing at Paul into visionary language connected to "the Lord sitting like Paul" (21). Since sitting is a teaching posture (Matt 5:1; 23:2; 26:55; John 8:2), her gaze concerns divine revelation: Paul's teachings as revelatory are placed in relation to the Lord's teachings. Thecla consistently desires Paul's revelatory teaching.

---

[13] McLarty, *Thecla's Devotion*, 92.
[14] For further discussion of the description of Paul, see chapter 5.
[15] Eyl, "Why Thecla Does not See Paul."

Conspicuous in their absence, the *ATh* has no pirates, a typical element in all romances. The main characters always encounter pirates on their journey. Pirates are so elemental to the genre that they occur, albeit briefly, even in *DC* (1.28–30), which takes place almost exclusively on the island of Lesbos. The pirates instigate the brief journey off the island; in that way, *DC* incorporates two central motifs of the genre. This omission of pirates from the *ATh* is easily accounted for by the fact that Iconium is located inland, away from the Mediterranean Sea. When Thecla travels, she does so on foot.

Finally, the *ATh* lacks the motif of suicidal grief. Threats of suicide are common in the romances whenever a lover is faced with becoming unchaste or losing the beloved (*ET* 2.4, 7; *Call* 5.10; 6.2, 6; 7.1; *LC* 7.6). For instance, when Antheia (*ET* 5.8) becomes enslaved to a brothel keeper, she contemplates taking her own life, despondent that she faces the constant threat of being forced into prostitution. She says, "It is best for me to die nobly with my chastity intact." The closest parallel occurs in the *ATh* when Thecla throws herself into the water (34): The women and the entire crowd weep and tell her not to do it. Thecla throws herself into the water in an act of self-baptism, apparently because she does not want to die without having been baptized. The *ATh*, however, maintains the overwhelming concern for Thecla's purity.

Further reading on the relation between the *ATh* and the romances: Calef, "Thecla 'Tried and True' and the Inversion of Romance"; McLarty, *Thecla's Devotion*; Esch-Wermeling, *Thekla — Paulusschülerin wider Willen? Strategien der Leserlenkung in den Theklaakten*; Cooper, *The Virgin and the Bride: Idealized Womanhood in Late Antiquity*; Perkins, *The Suffering Self: Pain and Narrative Representation in the Early Christian Era*. Calef reads the *ATh* as an adventure novel of ordeal in which the hero undergoes a test of endurance, variations of which occur in the Greek romances and Jewish and Christian literature. McLarty focuses on parallels between the *ATh* and *Call*. Esch-Wermeling analyzes parallels between *ATh* and *ET*. Cooper and Perkins offer seminal readings of the *ATh* in light of the romances. See also Appendix 2: Homer's *Odyssey* and Euripides's *Hippolytus*.

Chapter 3

Patronage and Related Imagery
in the *Acts of Thecla*

There is much about the Greco-Roman world that is foreign to us in the twenty-first century. This chapter focuses on one cultural phenomenon of the Greco-Roman world that the original hearers of the *ATh* took for granted: the patron-client system. First, we will introduce how that system typically operated and then demonstrate ways in which patronage provides background to the narrative plot and theology of the *ATh*. We will also introduce the closely related image of *paterfamilias*, which plays a vital role in the *ATh*. This way of reading the *ATh* is certainly not the only approach, but we hope you find it useful for delving into the story in a way that approximates how the original audience may have related to the story and its message.

A Brief Overview of Patronage

The English words "patron" and "client" today have meanings related to the advent of capitalism in the sixteenth century. Today a patron is someone who patronizes a store or restaurant, while a client is someone with whom one transacts some sort of business exchange. In the context of the Greco-Roman world, these words have different meanings. What is referred to as "the patron-client system" was a reciprocal relationship between two people of unequal social standing: a patron was a powerful, wealthy person who did favors for people who were not as high in the social system; the person for whom the patron did a favor was called a client, and these clients in turn were indebted to the patron to return favors when asked. Virtually everyone in the Greco-Roman world was both a patron and a client, with the emperor (Caesar) being the highest patron. A Roman senator could be a patron to many clients while still being a client to one or more patrons. All it took was being indebted to someone for something such as helping achieve a position in the Senate or buying a home or marrying someone of high social rank. Patronage was vital for moving goods and services around and up and down through social rank.[1] As David deSilva writes, "patronage was an essential means of acquiring access to goods, protection, or opportunities for employment and advancement."[2]

It was common in Rome for the clients to perform a duty called *salutatio* (greeting) in which the client would go to the home of the patron to show gratitude, seek advice, and be available should the patron require some service. Whether that custom was also done throughout the Greco-Roman world is unclear, but the duty of the client to show gratitude for the patron's beneficence was pervasive. The patronage system regulated daily life of the Greco-Roman world and was a way in which people had protection against violence. With few exceptions, there was no police in the Greco-Roman world. Instead, people relied on kinship connections and the patronage network. Since people knew who a person's patron was, it was understood that harming or dishonoring someone could garner reprisal from the person's patron as well as kin. There is considerable evidence that women were also patrons (or matrons).

Another aspect of the patron-client system concerned the middleman, who served as mediator or broker between patrons or between a patron and other clients. To be a mediator or broker could simply mean that a patron sent you on an errand to communicate the patron's wishes, as is the case in Luke 7:1–10, in which a Gentile centurion who has acted as patron for the local Jewish community sends Jewish elders, his clients, to ask a favor of Jesus. In that case, the clients serve as brokers or mediators.

---

[1] For a recent discussion of patronage in the Roman monetary system, see Elliott, *Economic Theory and the Roman Monetary Economy*.

[2] DeSilva, *Honor*, 96.

In summary, every free citizen and freed person in the Greco-Roman world was enmeshed in the patron-client system for social advancement, protection, and to do business.[3] People had to pay attention to and find out a person's social rank, family connections, and patron-client associations. Mediation between patrons was done through clients or other lower-ranked patrons who acted as brokers. We now turn to two instances in the plot of the *ATh* where the ancient audience would likely have understood the situation from patron-client dynamics: Alexander's actions to acquire Thecla through Paul (26) and Tryphaena's care for Thecla in her home (30). Both of these instances concern patronage as a means of protection.

For introductory overviews of patronage, see: Matyszak, *24 Hours in Ancient Rome: A Day in the Life of People who Lived There*, "Hora I"; deSilva, "Patronage"; Elliott, "Patronage and Clientage." Regarding Luke 7:1–10, see Malina and Rohrbaugh, *Social-Science Commentary on the Synoptic Gospels*, 252 and 390; cf. Wheatley, *Patronage in Early Christianity: Its Use and Transformation from Jesus to Paul of Samosata*.

Paul's Refusal to Protect Thecla in the Antioch Scene (26)

Before we delve into how patron-broker-client imagery operates in the *ATh* in theological ways, we will first examine how the patron-client system helps to better comprehend the dynamics of the plot concerning the exchange between Paul and Alexander and the relationship between Thecla and Tryphaena.

The scene approaching Antioch in which Paul puts Thecla in grave peril by telling Alexander that she is not "his" is perhaps the most discussed passage in the *ATh*. We do not claim to have "the" answer to interpreting this passage, but we can provide the contours of the debate, share our perspectives, and invite you to form your own view.

---

[3] Freedmen were clients to their former owners. Even noncitizens were required to have a patron (deSilva, *Honor,* 103). Although slaves were more restricted from receiving the benefits of social advancement within patronage, they served as mediators, among other roles, and there was a hierarchy among the enslaved. See Weaver, *Familia Caesaris*; López Barja de Quiroga, "Patronage and Slavery in the Roman World."

It is crucial to notice that Alexander approaches Paul about acquiring Thecla. Greco-Roman culture assumes that a woman in an itinerant group is embedded in the house of a male *paterfamilias* within the group (see the box below). Alexander therefore assumes that Thecla is Paul's wife, concubine, or slave, and so he inquires about her through Paul. Also, important is that Alexander desires Thecla for her beauty. The text does not tell us how she is dressed, but we know from the story that her hair is not shaved. The story is indebted to the Greek romance tradition of love at first sight. Alexander's lust for Thecla ("he desired her intensely") results in efforts to acquire her through Paul with wealth and gifts. Paul's words, "I do not know the woman of whom you speak nor is she mine," require some unpacking. Greek manuscript 50 reads that he does not know "this (woman) as you say."[4] In one sense, Paul is telling the truth: Thecla is not his, as he is neither the head of her household nor her patron. The verb "know" in this context almost certainly has the connotation of "being *intimately* acquainted with," and so Paul tells Alexander that he does not have intercourse with Thecla. It is inaccurate, however, that he does not "know" Thecla in the sense of knowing who she is, "know" in the sense of being acquainted with. This double sense of "know" makes Paul's disavowal of her insidious insofar as the first sense of "know," intimate acquaintance, could lead a man to assume that Thecla is not an honorable woman — she is a woman about whom men can speak freely without repercussion.

The problems that this passage occasions become obvious by examining the explanatory additions introduced in the Greek manuscripts and other versions of the *A Th*: A Syriac form of the *A Th* adds, "if she is a woman as you say." In that version, Paul's puzzling denial of knowing Thecla (acquainted with or intimately) is thereby turned into a dissimilatory ruse to protect her and is part of the notion that Thecla is in disguise.[5] The Coptic similarly adds a

---

[4] We are grateful to Willy Rordorf for emailing the critical apparatus of this verse from the forthcoming critical edition.

[5] Paul's disavowal of Thecla also caused some embarrassment or discomfort in the fifth-century *Life of Thecla* attributed to Basil of Seleucia (Pseudo-Basil),

clarification that presupposes a sexual connotation for "to know": "I do not know this woman *as a wife*."[6] The most difficult and therefore most likely original reading is "I do not know the woman of whom you speak" without additional clarification.

Even without such later additions aimed at clarifying a difficult text, the most likely original reading still presents problems of interpretation. The forthcoming Greek edition reads, "I do not know this woman in the way that you say," following manuscript 50 and other versions. An indication that the text is unclear is that the editors intervene to explain the translation in a footnote: "Paul purposely exposes Thecla to a new trial in order to give her an occasion of triumph."[7] Their understanding—that Paul is deliberately exposing her to a new trial—is possible but not explicit in the text.[8] This common way of reading the passage tends to take Paul's words in 25, "Another trial will overtake you, worse than the first, and you may not endure [it] but behave cowardly," as a premonition or forewarning based on the notion that she is not yet ready for baptism. While that is one way of reading the text, the implied author and the original listeners would not necessarily have been predisposed to a positive understanding of Paul's behavior in this scene despite the otherwise positive depictions of him elsewhere in the story. A negative (or not entirely positive) reaction to Paul's words and inaction may well have been an option in Greco-Roman cultural context, as will soon be clear.

The moment Paul disclaims her, Alexander "with considerable strength, embraced her in the street." Alexander's conduct is an assault, a use of force without consent. Paul does nothing when this happens. The effect of Paul's words and inaction is that Alexander assumes Thecla is an itinerant woman without *paterfamilias* or

---

which reworks the scene. See Johnson, *Life and Miracles*, 45–48; Dagron, *Vie et Miracles*, 231.

[6] As in many languages, the Coptic word for "woman" and "wife" are the same.

[7] Rordorf with Cherix and Kasser, trans., "Actes de Paul," 1137. The phrase "And she made him into a laughing-stock" uses the word *thriambon*, which can carry an allusion to a Roman general's triumph.

[8] Cf. 1 Timothy 3:10 that *diakonous*, male and female ministers, should be tested first.

patron to protect her, as Paul has neither claimed her nor defended her. Strongly implied is that Alexander assumes that she is a slave, a prostitute, or both, and she is therefore without honor or recourse to stop him.

Box 3: Paterfamilias

Paterfamilias, from Latin, literally meaning father + family, or male of head of household, is a term used as a shorthand for the organization of the household around a male father figure who exercised enormous power (*patria potestas*, "paternal power") over the people and goods within the home, clan, or tribe. There is no exact Greek equivalent, but *paterfamilias* encapsulates key aspects of the Greco-Roman head of household. The texts that concern household management, as Osiek and MacDonald explain, are primarily prescriptive, not descriptive, as marriage, divorce, death, remarriage, half-siblings, step-children, and reversal of fortunes changed the dynamics of a household.[9] For women, being embedded in a household with a *paterfamilias* was critical for safety, even though the male head of household exercised ultimate control over subordinate members. The *paterfamilias* role was closely related to that of patron.[10]

Further reading: Joubert, "Managing the Household: Paul as *Paterfamilias* of the Christian Household group in Corinth"; White, "Paul and *Pater Familias*"; Arjava, "Paternal Power in Late Antiquity."

In the *ATh*, as in Mark's Gospel and John's Gospel, the heroes of the story have no human father and the texts stress that God is father (Mark 14:36; John 5:36–37; 10:29–30; *ATh* 6, 24). Thecla lays claim to God as both Jesus's father and her father (24). Regarding the effects of the patriarchal God-imagery on spiritual imaginations and gender roles, see Schneiders, *Women and the Word*; O'Day, "Gospel of John," 529–30.

---

[9] Osiek and MacDonald, *A Woman's Place*, 17–23.
[10] White, "Paul and *Pater Familias*," 471.

When Alexander grabs at her (26), Thecla makes three appeals in quick succession—first, to the Greco-Roman cultural code of honoring the stranger. In doing so, she reminds Alexander that Zeus is the protector of strangers and exacts revenge against those who violate a stranger. Second, she asserts that she is "the slave of God." This statement is ambiguous. Although "slave of God" can be understood as a reference to the Christian God, she does not actually specify the god; therefore, Alexander would have heard it as an appeal for him to recognize that to mistreat a slave of a god is to dishonor that god.[11] This statement is perhaps also a warning to avoid property violation since Roman law prohibited raping or abducting someone else's slave.[12] Finally, she appeals to her elite status in Iconium, letting him know that she is not a slave devoid of family honor and modesty. In her aggressive counterattack, she marshals a series of defenses, any of which Paul could have made on her behalf but did not. In the previous scene (25), Paul had expressed concern that Thecla may face another test "worse than the first" that she will be unable to endure. Paul's concern for her safety in that scene evaporates when Alexander attacks her. Paul's inaction sets into motion the trial that Paul had warned could happen. Not only is it far from clear that the implied author intends the audience to understand that Paul allowed this assault to take place so that Thecla would undergo another trial, but also some in the original audience may well have seen Paul's conduct as deeply troubling for an honorable male in that culture, as this scene depicts Paul as passive and helpless in the public arena.

After making those three appeals with no assistance from Paul, Thecla then defends herself physically. Her self-defense, though vigorous, does not go to the extent of Antheia's use of a sword to kill the man attacking her (*ET* 4.5). Since Alexander was a priest of the imperial cult, her attack on his garments would be understood as hostility toward imperial authority, an authority that is aligned with the imperial cult. The crown that she took from his head likely had

---

[11] Pervo, *The Acts of Paul*, 149.

[12] McGinn, *Prostitution, Sexuality and the Law in Ancient Rome*, 313–32.

the image of the emperor on it, a detail added in the Armenian and some Syriac forms of the story.[13]

Interpretation of this scene is quite disputed, but for the most part scholars either offer various reasons Paul does not come to Thecla's defense or they see Paul being depicted as cowardly and passive. Richard Pervo argues that Paul's denial of Thecla "liberates" her[14] and is therefore an affirmation of "no male and female" (Gal 3:28) in which Paul rejects sexual differentiation.[15] Margaret MacDonald reads the text through the social values of honor and shame, noting that "Thecla assumes the offensive stance of the male guardian and protects her own honour" and that "by defending herself with strength and courage, Thecla has assumed the traditional role of the male in the public honour context."[16] Just as this scene is often read as part of the feminization of Paul, it is also read as the increasing masculinization of Thecla.[17] McLarty sees both Alexander and Thecla as transgressing boundaries: Alexander through a display of immoral lack of self-mastery in his uncontrolled desire and Thecla for traveling with a man unrelated to her.[18] A strength of this interpretation is that it coheres with the view found in the Greek romance *Callirhoe* that using force shows a lack of self-control or moderation (2.6). We suggest another possible reading that takes into consideration the entirety of the *ATh*: This compromising depiction of Paul serves the larger purpose of driving home a major theological point of the *ATh*, that Paul is not Thecla's patron; he is mediator and instigator of her faith, but God-Christ is Thecla's patron and *paterfamilias* who delivers her from her trials

---

[13] Price, *Rituals and Power*, 124. Pervo, *The Acts of Paul*, 157, provides helpful contemporary analogies: assaulting the color-bearer at a Memorial Day parade and a bishop during a Corpus Christi procession. (Both analogies are required, as there was no separation of religion and state in the Greco-Roman world.)

[14] Pervo, *The Acts of Paul*, 149.

[15] Pervo, *The Acts of Paul*, 152.

[16] MacDonald, *Early Christian Women*, 175–76.

[17] There is further discussion of feminization and masculinization of characters in chapter 5.

[18] McLarty, *Thecla's Devotion*, 208. For additional readings of this scene, see Kraemer, *Unreliable Witnesses*, 141–42; Andrious, *Saint Thecla*, 116–17; Vorster, "Construction of Culture Through the Construction of Person," 115.

and brings about her salvation (42). The ambiguous depiction of Paul in the *ATh* is perhaps foreshadowed by Onesiphoros's description of his physical appearance (3), which can be read as a mix of positive and negative attributes (cf. chapter 5, pp. 93–95, on "How do you understand the physical description of Paul?")

In the *ATh*, Alexander continually tries to reassert his dominance over Thecla and to re-establish himself as honorable after their initial meeting. When Alexander succeeds in getting Thecla thrown to the beasts, he effectively repudiates her claims to be elite and a slave of God insofar as in that culture the moment one is condemned to death in the arena, the person loses the status once held as a free elite, including citizenship, and is considered an actual slave without any claim to honor.[19] Alexander not only fails to see that Thecla is an honorable woman, but he also fails to see where power and honor truly derive. This portrayal of Alexander in relation to Thecla's resilience throughout the sufferings Alexander inflicts on her points to a paradox of power and honor in the story. Despite Alexander's civic power and the honor status it brings, his power is no match for Thecla's God. Moreover, Alexander is incorrect that Thecla does not belong to any household and therefore is without protection and honor. Thecla, chaste and exhibiting incredible endurance, is embedded in the household of God as the slave of God, eventually becoming a mediator like Paul in her own right.

Tryphaena's Patronage and Maternal Roles

In strong contrast to Paul's lack of patronage, the *ATh* provides Thecla with an important human patron, Tryphaena, who is depicted as powerfully connected to the Roman imperial family. Tryphaena acts as Thecla's patron when she allows her to stay in her home instead of facing the prospect of losing her chastity in prison. Tryphaena's power is particularly evident when she turns Alexander away when he comes to bring Thecla to the arena (30). That action is not inconsequential, as Alexander himself is a powerful patron as head of the provincial council and organizer of

---

[19] Fagan, *The Lure of the Arena*, 174–75.

the animal games. The *quid pro quo* arrangement of patronage—I do something for you, you do something for me—is evident here when Tryphaena saves Thecla's chastity by taking her into her home.[20] Thecla becomes indebted to Tryphaena and will need to be available should her patron request something. Thus, when Tryphaena asks Thecla to mediate her daughter's journey in the afterlife, Thecla does so. Tryphaena also acts as a surrogate mother to Thecla when she refers to Thecla as "my second child" (29) and "my child" (30, twice). The maternal role plays out further when Thecla becomes Tryphaena's heir (39: "I will put in writing [that] all my property is for you"). Tryphaena's maternal and patronage roles coexist side by side in the *A Th*.[21]

While Tryphaena has the crucially important role of protecting Thecla from being shamed through rape in prison, she does not have the power to reverse the shame of the mother's condemnation (20). Only God's patronage, as discussed below, provides Thecla with that affirmation of honor despite Theocleia's claims to the contrary implied in her condemnation. Thecla credits divine intervention for saving her from the shame of being seen naked (38), while in the arena, "The one who clothes my nakedness among the beasts, He will clothe me with salvation on the Day of Judgment." We now turn to patronage as a lens to view theology, first in the larger Pauline tradition and then in the *A Th*.

Further reading on Tryphaena and matronage: Misset-van de Weg, "A Wealthy Woman named Tryphaena"; Misset-van de Weg "Answers to the Plights of an Ascetic Woman Named Thecla"; Osiek and MacDonald, *A Woman's Place*, ch. 7 and ch. 9.

---

[20] The logic of patronage is also exemplified in the Greek romance *Callirhoe* when the pirates discuss what to do with Callirhoe, whom they discovered alive in the tomb they were robbing. One pirate suggests (*Call* 1.10) that they return her to her husband and thereby will be considered her patrons who saved her from death and will receive many gifts from the wealthy family.

[21] Regarding Tryphaena's patronage in the Pauline tradition, see Cooper, *Band of Angels*, 8–10. On Tryphaena's maternal role, see Kraemer, *Unreliable Witnesses*, 133; Cohick, "Mothers, Martyrs, and Manly Courage"; McLarty, *Thecla's Devotion*, 183–87.

Paul's Use of Patron-Broker-Client Rhetoric

There are several reasons to examine patronage imagery as background for understanding the theology and story of the *ATh*. The author of the *ATh* would have wanted to draw on such imagery because it was familiar to an audience brought up in a culture that took for granted the patron-client system. In addition, patronage language was employed in reference to the gods in the Greco-Roman world, particularly in terms of the divine benefits that the gods bring to humans. For instance, Aristides, a second-century CE devotee of the healing god Asclepius, composed an oration on Asclepius in which he refers to the god as his patron (33.2) and praises him for the benefits he provides (33.17; 42.5).[22] Finally, the author of the *ATh* would have been aware of the patronage imagery in the New Testament and presumably would have been familiar with Paul's patronage imagery. To take one example, in 2 Corinthians 1:3, Paul identifies God as the dispenser of benefactions through eulogistic ("blessing") statements: "Blessed [is] the God and Father of our Lord Jesus Christ" (also Eph 1:3; 1 Pet 1:3).[23] These statements, common also in the Hebrew Bible, praise God as dispenser of benefactions, an attribute of a patron that is sometimes coupled with *paterfamilias* imagery. A brief overview of patron-client imagery in Paul's letters supplies useful context for a closer examination of similar imagery in the *ATh*.

Paul operates as broker or mediator between God and the communities in Christ. Sometimes he explicitly employs such language, as is the case in 2 Corinthians 5:20, where he describes his role as broker in terms of a Roman diplomat (*legatus*), whose task was to keep the peace between Rome and the provinces.[24] Paul often indicates that God called him as an apostle, "one sent" (Rom 1:1; 1 Cor 1:1; 15:1–2); he states that his role as "one sent" is the will of God (2 Cor 1:1). As a result of visions and revelations, Paul has access to

---

[22] Johnson, *Among the Gentiles*, 58.

[23] In *ATh* 4, Onesiphoros calls God blessed, and we find the almost identical description of God as Father in relation to Jesus in *ATh* 25 ("the Father of our Lord Jesus Christ").

[24] Joubert, "Managing the Household," 216.

mystical heavenly experience (2 Cor 12:1-6), and he proclaims the "mystery of God" (1 Cor 2:1). He and Sosthenes speak "God's wisdom, mysterious, hidden" (1 Cor 2:7). In Galatians, an aspect of God's patronage is the outpouring of the Spirit (3:5; 4:6-7), considered a gift of God, an element lacking in the patronage background to the *A Th* but present in the Acts of the Apostles (Acts 11:15-18) and in the rest of the *Acts of Paul*.[25]

It is common to analyze biblical texts through the lens of the patron-client system. Further reading: deSilva, *Honor, Patronage, Kinship and Purity*; Lampe, "Paul, Patrons, and Clients," esp. 505-7; Neyrey, *Render to God: New Testament Understandings of the Divine*.

Divine Patronage in the *A Th*: God's Saving Compassion for Thecla

The narrator indicates that God's powerful beneficence toward Thecla is grounded in "compassion" (22). As already noted, Thecla credits divine intervention for saving her from the shame of being seen naked (38) while in the arena. The shame of public nudity was a matter of social status, the context in which the nudity occurs, and is related to the ability of the elite *paterfamilias* to protect the women of his home from public shame through exposure.[26] In crediting God in this way, Thecla depicts God as fulfilling the role that Greco-Roman culture took for granted as the unique purview of a powerful *paterfamilias*. We should not be surprised, therefore, to find that Thecla lays claim to God as her father (24). Although the *paterfamilias* and patron roles were distinct insofar as the latter concerned those outside the family, the roles coalesced in the head of household. God's compassion in the *A Th* extends remarkably beyond the Christian household to include a dead person who was never baptized, Falconilla (28-29). As the "foundation of eternal life" (37), Christ acts as would a patron who grants the mediator's request on behalf of another person, in this case Thecla's request for Falconilla's transfer to the place of the righteous.

---

[25] The *A Th* twice refers to grace (God's favor): once in describing Paul (3) and once in a greeting (4). Regarding grace, see deSilva, *Honor*, ch. 4.

[26] Brown, *Body and Society*, 315-16.

When Thecla testifies to what has happened to her at the end of the story, she is grateful for Tryphaena's motherly love and patronage, but she credits Jesus, whom she calls God, for her salvation (42): "O Christ Jesus, the Son of God, my helper when I was in prison, helper in the presence of governors, helper in the fire, helper against the beasts. You indeed are God. And to you is the glory forever and ever, Amen." The language she uses here, calling Jesus "helper" four times, would have been understood by a Greco-Roman audience as assigning Jesus the role of broker or mediator between God and the client, similar to Christ's mediator role in 1 Timothy 2:5 and Hebrews 8:6; 9:5; and 12:24. As with the high christology of the Epistle to the Hebrews in which the Son is referred to as God (Heb 1:8–9) while maintaining Jesus's role of mediator, so Thecla's prayer combines Jesus's mediating role as "helper" while explicitly identifying Jesus as God.

Clients and Mediators in the *ATh*

A Greco-Roman audience would have understood Paul in the *ATh* as God's client who praises his patron, God, as a client should (24). His role as God's client is also affirmed when Onesiphoros greets Paul by calling him God's slave (4). Paul calls Jesus "Lord" (24), which demonstrates both Paul's client role and also the close connection between God and Jesus in the *ATh*. Moreover, Paul's role as client extends to mediation: Paul dutifully mediates, acts as broker, between God and the people when he states, "I teach the things revealed to me by God" (17). The teachings in Paul's beatitudes (5–6) convey what pleases the divine patron and the favors bestowed as a result of complying to the patron's wishes. Paul's role as apostle, one "sent out" to evangelize (spread the good news), is made explicit in his defense speech before the proconsul of Iconium (17), where he states that a living God who desires salvation sent him to save humanity from destruction, impurity, every pleasure, and death. Paul is the mediator who leads Thecla to the Christian faith (5–7), and he prays for Thecla to be rescued from the fire (24).[27] However, in the pyre scene (22), the narrator credits God for saving Thecla from the fire, and Thecla herself reiterates that point (24) when she comes upon Paul praying for her in the tomb. It is not just that there may be a deliberate comic element to the tomb scene, but that the story emphasizes that God-Christ saves, not Paul, who acts as God's mediator.

Paul's lofty mediating role as teacher in the *ATh* is affirmed in several ways, including when the narrative connects Paul to Jesus: At 17, Paul states that God sent him, which leads him to assert that God sent Jesus, his son, "whom I preach and teach that in Him humanity has hope who alone has shown compassion for a wayward world, so that humans are no longer subject to judgment but have faith and fear of God and knowledge of dignified behavior and love of truth." Paul's teaching role is also emphasized in connection to Jesus at 21 in Thecla's mystical vision of "the Lord sitting like Paul." Finally, the *ATh* always refers to Paul teaching "the word of God" (5, 39, 40) or "the word of the Father" (6) or "the word of Christ" (7), but paragraph 10 refers to Thecla relentlessly listening to "the word of Paul": "Thecla would not be turned away, but kept observing closely the word of Paul."

As a result of hearing Paul teaching, Thecla's greatest desire in the *ATh* is to acquire "the seal in Christ" (25), that is, baptism, which will finalize her role as God's client and facilitate her role as broker on the patron's behalf. The language of "seal" (*sphrangida*) is the same word for the "signet ring" that the patron allowed a trusted client to use on his behalf in doing the patron's bidding as broker.[28] Even before she baptizes herself (34), Thecla calls God "Lord" (31) and identifies as God's slave (26), important client designations that she repeats post-baptism (37: "I am slave of the living God"; 43: "the Lord lives"). She shows proper gratitude to the patron who saved

---

[27] It is not entirely clear, however, that Paul acts as mediator of Thecla's rescue from the fire. The text may imply so when a boy tells Thecla (23) that Paul has been praying and fasting for six days, "for he sighs deeply for you." The prayer Paul is saying (24) may be understood as the sort of prayer he has been performing those past six days.

[28] See also Haggai 2:23 (LXX): "'I will make you like a signet ring [*sphrangida*], for I have chosen you,' says the Lord of Hosts"; cf. John 6:27.

66

her, Jesus, whom she calls "helper," as noted above, four times in her prayer at 42. As Paul had done, so also Thecla praises God for what God has done (24).

As client who acts as a broker, Thecla beseeches God's favor on behalf of Tryphaena's dead daughter (29), mediating Falconilla's transfer to the place of the righteous on behalf of her human patron, Tryphaena, which returns the favor Tryphaena had done in saving her purity and consoling her (27); it also puts Tryphaena in debt to Thecla in a reciprocal relationship. One role of the patron is to promote the upward mobility of the client,[29] which Thecla facilitates through her connection with the patron Jesus. The story depicts Thecla as client-mediator with connections to a powerful patron, just as Paul was depicted at the beginning of the narrative. The text also depicts Thecla as mediator of Tryphaena's wealth to Paul.[30]

An additional plausible indication of Thecla's role as God's client is the "power" evident in her when the governor sees her nude (22): "When she was brought in, naked, the governor wept and he was amazed at the power in her." Although the governor probably sees her as displaying power through endurance, the power in Thecla is a strong parallel with the power in Jesus in the Gospels (Mark 5:30; Luke 6:19; 10:19), the power of Christ that dwells in Paul (2 Cor 12:9), and God's power demonstrated through human beings (Rom 9:17). As client and mediator, the patron's power extends to Thecla. That the governor does not grasp the deeper theological significance of Thecla's power in the way the original audience, made up of Christians, may well have, is an instance of situational irony in the narrative.[31]

The narrative indicates through the word "faith" (7 and 18), which in a patron-client context refers to loyalty, trust, and dependability,[32] that Thecla's loyalty toward the divine patron grows over the course of the narrative, culminating in her itinerant

---

[29] Lampe, "Paul, Patrons, and Clients," 506.

[30] Interestingly, Thecla's role as mediator of Tryphaena's financial support is removed in the Heidelberg Coptic, wherein her support goes directly to Paul.

[31] On situational irony in the *ATh*, see Aubin, "Reversing Romance."

[32] DeSilva, *Honor*, 115; Lampe, "Paul, Patrons, and Clients," 506.

apostolic teaching (43) in imitation of and with the blessing of her teacher Paul (41). When testifying to her mother, Thecla attempts to broker a relationship between her mother and "a Lord" who lives in heaven (43) and "a Lord" (Lipsius's reading) who will grant wealth to her mother through her. The latter reading—"a Lord will give it [wealth] to you through me"—is ambiguous, perhaps deliberately so; it can refer to Thecla as offering to broker wealth between God and her mother (wealth in an expansive sense, including the good news) and also between a human patron and her mother (including material wealth). The Greek word *kyrios*, often translated as "Lord," was a common term of address for a human patron that was also applied to divine patrons. The original reading, however, seems to be "God will give it to you through me" (see Appendix 1), which specifies divine patronage with an emphasis on Thecla as mediator of spiritual wealth, the good news.[33] Significantly, Thecla's role as broker is emphasized in the narrative's final line, which states that she enlightened "many" (43). Her role as broker of the faith is the concluding statement of the *ATh*.

Summary

The *ATh* contains a variety of implied understandings of the characters when viewed from the cultural contexts of patronage and head of household. God is Thecla's patron and *paterfamilias* who delivers her, providing salvation. Christ is God, patron, and also mediator between God and humanity. Paul is God's client and mediator who reveals God's message, which is also Christ's message. Paul mediates God's teachings to Thecla, but he disavows the patron and *paterfamilias* roles when Alexander attempts to acquire her through him, which puts her in grave danger and results in the trial that Paul had feared might come (25).

---

[33] The forthcoming critical edition of the Greek (Appendix 1), in contrast to the Lipsius edition, reads *ho theos* (God) in this clause instead of *kyrios* (Lord): "God will give them [riches] to you through me." We are grateful to Willy Rordorf for sending us the critical apparatus of this verse: Twice as many Greek manuscripts read "God," including manuscript 50, as do several versions, including the Latin. It would seem that the change from "God" to "Lord" was made in order to include human patronage.

Theologically crucial to the narrative is that God is Thecla's patron. The narrative goes to great lengths to emphasize that Paul is *not* her patron. The portrayal of Alexander points to a paradox of power in the story: Despite Alexander's power as patron of the civic games, his power is no match for God's patronage toward Thecla. Tryphaena is the human patron to Thecla in the narrative, and in turn she becomes a client on account of Thecla's mediating role in God's transfer of her daughter to the place of the righteous. Thecla is God's client and mediator, first to Tryphaena, and after her teacher Paul commissions her to "Go and teach the word of God" (41), Thecla as a teacher becomes mediator to many others, male and female (43), as was her mentor, Paul.

We have seen that scholars are divided over whether Paul in the *ATh* is depicted entirely positively or somewhat negatively. Since the matter is complicated, we will return to it again in chapter 5. In the next chapter, we address important ways in which the *ATh* is read in relation to the Pastoral Epistles.

Chapter 4

The *Acts of Thecla* and the Pastoral Epistles

The first two centuries of the Christ movement did not have uniform growth of principles and practice. Rather, there were different interpretations of the faith. Christ groups were interpreting the teachings, sayings, and stories of Jesus in a variety of ways; for instance, some emphasized Jewish roots more than others, some the ongoing inspiration of the holy Spirit, others a particular emphasis on the words and teachings of Jesus instead of his miraculous deeds. Just as there were multiple views on and points of emphasis about Jesus, so too with Paul, who was enormously influential.

An introduction to the *ATh* must contend with the fact that scholars often read it over against the Pastoral Epistles (PE). There are a variety of interesting ways to read these two works alongside each other, but our focus is on agreements between the *ATh* and 2 Timothy and tensions between the *ATh* and 1 Timothy 2:8–15. After a brief overview of the PE, we note broad connections between these works and then compare and contrast what each communicates about women's roles and salvation. A comparison with the PE as a whole is fascinating because the *ATh* shares names, themes, and larger concerns with 2 Timothy much more so than with 1 Timothy. Also interesting is that this juxtaposition reveals that nascent Christian communities were discussing women's roles and their salvation. Proper female behavior in relationship to salvation is a crucial point of tension between the *ATh* and 1 Timothy.

Studies of the *ATh* in relation to the PE in English include the following: Hylen, *A Modest Apostle: Thecla and the History of Women in the Early Church*; den Dulk, "I Permit No Woman to Teach except for Thecla"; Kraemer, *Unreliable Witnesses: Religion,*

Gender, and History in the Greco-Roman Mediterranean, ch. 4; Osiek and MacDonald, *A Woman's Place*; M. MacDonald, *Early Christian Women and Pagan Opinion: The Power of the Hysterical Woman*, part 2, esp. 154–82; Bassler, *1 Timothy, 2 Timothy, Titus*; Burrus, *Chastity and Autonomy: Women in the Stories of the Apocryphal Acts*; D. MacDonald, *The Legend and the Apostle: The Battle for Paul in Story and Canon*.

What are the Pastoral Epistles?

The Pastoral Epistles are three letters in the New Testament—1 Timothy, 2 Timothy, and Titus—that are attributed to Paul, although most scholars in the past two centuries have determined that they were almost certainly written by someone else in Paul's name, that is, pseudonymously.[1] Some scholars speculate that perhaps Paul made use of a secretary for these letters. Another possibility is that these three letters retain fragments of the historical Paul's writings that were then compiled and expanded upon in Paul's name at a later time. The vocabulary and other matters in the PE probably indicate that someone other than Paul composed these letters at least in their final forms. For instance, the seven genuine letters of the historical Paul, composed primarily in the 50s, show little concern for having and managing children (1 Tim 3:4, 12; 5:14). Since we do not know the name of the author, scholars sometimes refer to him as "the Pastor." We will continue that convention even though the PE differ in a variety of ways from each other.

Writing in someone's name, pseudonymity, in this case writing in Paul's name, was done out of respect and to appropriate the person's authority. The Pastor appropriates Paul's considerable authority to encourage his audience toward specific ways of conduct in light of the author's theological views and cultural presuppositions, which do not always neatly cohere with Paul's seven genuine letters. Exactly when the PE were composed is

---

[1] A study Bible will provide an overview of the disputed nature of the authorship in relation to the rest of the Pauline corpus. For a critique of the arguments for pseudonymity and unitary packaging of the PE, see Johnson, *The First and Second Letters to Timothy*, 20–99.

unclear, but they probably date to early in the second century, several decades before the *A Th*.[2] The Pastor addresses matters that arise for communities dealing with living in the Greco-Roman world for the long haul.

First Timothy is centrally concerned with what has traditionally been (through Martin Luther's influence) and still often is referred to as "household codes,"[3] that is, arrangements of the family household and proper conduct, parental and filial piety within the household of God (1 Tim 2:2; 3:15; 4:6; 6:6) in relation to "God's household plan" (1 Tim 1:4).[4] Scholars often point out that there is a common theme of subordination in the PE as the solution to many of the problems addressed:[5] women submitting to men, slaves submitting to masters, and community members submitting to the Pastor's teachings. These themes are not prevalent in 2 Timothy, however. First Timothy is particularly concerned with continuity in leadership and the succession of hierarchical roles within the growing movement.

While the PE are part of the Christian canon, and for that reason have significantly more authority today for Christians than the *A Th*, modern scholarship has found an important noncanonical voice in the *A Th* that counters some of the Pastor's perspectives, especially certain views expressed in 1 Timothy. We agree with those who find that it is helpful to read the *A Th* as a rejoinder to 1 Timothy 2:8–15 concerning appropriate roles for women and matters pertaining to salvation. Both texts advocate views regarding women's roles and

---

[2] For the date of the PE, see Collins, *1 & 2 Timothy and Titus*, 1–2; Pervo, *The Making of Paul*, 242.

[3] Some scholars today find the "household code" more aptly referred to as "household management." See Elliott, *1 Peter*, 503–11. Elliot notes that the household management model does a better job of taking into consideration Greco-Roman concern for order "in both the public and domestic realms that will ensure both the harmony and effective functioning of society and the favor of the gods." The *A Th* reflects this connection between the public and domestic realms when the matrons with children yell in support of Thecla (28).

[4] See Collins, *1 & 2 Timothy and Titus*, 54–59, 122–26, esp. excursus 2, "Christians in the World," and excursus 7, "Godliness."

[5] Bassler, *1 Timothy, 2 Timothy, Titus*, 24–31, 34; Martin, "1-2 Timothy and Titus," 421–22.

salvation while seeking to persuade their audiences by means of appropriating Paul's authority.

It is clear that the *A Th* knew about the PE; less clear is whether the Pastor knew about the *A Th* in the forms that it has come down to us. It is possible, but unverifiable, that the Pastor was acquainted to some extent with some aspect of the Thecla story, perhaps in oral form, but such a conclusion remains speculative.[6] We have not found any evidence that the Pastor is responding to the *A Th*. We do, however, find compelling connections to 2 Timothy and strong disconnects with 1 Timothy that lead us to conclude that the *A Th* engaged with the PE as part of its creative composition. The *A Th* communicates its theological vision in reaction to 1 Timothy while making use of 2 Timothy and the Greek romance genre.

Common Values, Themes, Names, and Locations

There are many interesting connections between the *A Th* and 2 Timothy in particular. Both value endurance in the face of persecution: 2 Tim 1:8; 2:3, 10; 3:10–11; 4:5 // *A Th* 21, 25. Both find problematic the view that resurrection has already taken place: 2 Tim 2:17–18 (attributed to Hymenaeus and Philetus) // *A Th* 14 (attributed to Demas and Hermogenes).

Scholars routinely note that the *A Th* and 2 Timothy share several names and locations, which the chart below illustrates. We are in general agreement with Matthijs den Dulk, who argues that these commonalities, all from 2 Timothy, are part of a larger pattern in which the *A Th* agrees with 2 Timothy and is in contention with 1 Timothy in important ways.[7]

---

[6] See MacDonald, *The Legend and the Apostle.*
[7] Den Dulk, "I Permit No Woman to Teach."

Subject	Pastoral Epistles	Thecla Narrative
Paul	Presented as the writer of 1 and 2 Timothy, addressed to Timothy	Primary missionary and Thecla's teacher; he affirms Thecla's teaching ministry: "Go and teach the Word of God" (41)
Titus	Recipient of the third letter of the PE; mentioned in 2 Timothy 4:10	Onesiphoros looking for Paul based on a description from Titus (2)
Onesiphoros	His family is mentioned positively (2 Tim 1:16–18; 4:19)	Host to Paul in Iconium (2–5); follows Paul when he is expelled from the city (23–26); host to Thecla at the end of the narrative (42)
Demas	Presented negatively as "enamored of the present world" and having deserted Paul (2 Tim 4:9–10)	Introduced as a hypocrite (1); tells Thamyris to bring Paul before the governor (11–14)
Hermogenes	Presented negatively as having deserted Paul (2 Tim 1:15)	Introduced as a hypocrite (1); tells Thymaris to bring Paul before the governor (11–14)

Subject	Pastoral Epistles	Thecla Narrative
Iconium and Antioch	"You have followed my teaching, way of life, purpose, faith, patience, love, endurance, persecutions, and sufferings, such as happened to me in Antioch, Iconium, and Lystra, persecutions I endured. Yet from all these things the Lord delivered me" (2 Tim 3:10–11).	The first chapter of the *A Th* is in Iconium (1–25). The second part of the *A Th* is in Antioch (26–43). These are chapters 3–4 of the *AP*.

Notice that it is not simply a shared list of names and locations, but the character assessments associated with the names also cohere. None of the characters are portrayed as positive in one text yet negative in the other. Hermogenes is presented in a negative light in the PE and as an antagonist in the *A Th*. Onesiphoros and his family are referred to positively in both texts. While there are also interesting points of agreement between 1 Timothy and the *A Th*, as noted below, the main area of conflict between the two concerns women's roles and behavior.

Some connections, however, are unclear: 2 Timothy 4:14–15 mentions an Alexander negatively as strongly resisting Christian preaching, which makes one wonder, based on all the other shared names, whether the name Alexander was chosen for the character who attacks Thecla based on a negative association. However, Alexander was a common name, and he appears to have been a Christian (1 Tim 1:20), so any direct association remains speculative.[8]

---

[8] There are additional negative association with this name. Alexander was the Greek name for Paris, who abducted Menelaus' wife, Helen, the most egregious violation of *xenia* (sacred duties of guest toward host) in Greek literature. Cf. *Iliad*

Moreover, there is not complete uniformity between the names: Demas and Hermogenes do not appear together in the PE; other names, such as Tryphaena, appear in Paul's genuine letters (Rom 16:12).

Although there are differences in the application of social norms and theology between the *A Th* and the other two PE, the points of thematic agreement often do not receive sufficient attention. For instance, the *A Th* and 1 Timothy and Titus agree on the following points:

- Both value purity (*agneia, agna*): 1 Timothy 4:12; 5:2, 22; Titus 2:5 // *A Th* 6, 7, 27.
- Both value dignified behavior: 1 Timothy 2:2; 3:4, 8 // *A Th* 17.
- Both value self-control: Titus 1:8, the importance of self-control (*egkrate*) for an overseer ("bishop")[9] // *A Th* 5, self-control (*egkrateia*) is identified as the heart of "Paul's message."[10] See Box 1 on "The Importance of Self-Control" in chapter 1. Both inherited this value from the Greco-Roman culture and the historical Paul. For Paul, self-mastery is one of the fruits of the Spirit (Gal 5:22–24) and is involved in

---

3.328–450; Aeschylus, *Agamemnon* 362–402. The *A Th*, however, gives no hint of this association.

[9] Overseer ("bishop" in NAB) was an administrative role in a Greco-Roman association.

[10] The *A Th* and the PE, however, employ distinct vocabulary regarding self-control as proper behavior. As Pervo and others note, the *A Th* proclaims *enkrateia* (self-control), while the Pastor has a particular emphasis on devotion, proper conduct and living, and acting devoutly (*eusebeia*) that is not present in the vocabulary of the *A Th* (*The Acts of Paul*, 101). In addition, the Pastor differentiates self-control by gender, employing the word *sophrosyne* with a nuance of "modesty" when applied to the control of women and expectations about the proper conduct of married women (1 Tim 2:9, 15: *sophrosyne* of women; 2 Tim 1:7: *sophrosyne* a gift of the holy Spirit; Titus 2:6, 9: *sophrosyne* of older and younger men). When *sophrosyne* is a male virtue, it concerns moderation of a variety of passions. In the Greek romances, *sophrosyne* often refers to the female maintaining "chastity," sexual self-control, while separated from her beloved. The *A Th* never employs the word *sophrosyne*, although it is extremely important in the Greek romances and in the PE.

attaining the ultimate goal, an imperishable wreath (1 Cor 9:24–27).

- Both use the phrase "slave of God": Titus 1:1; cf. 2 Timothy 2:24–25: "slave of the Lord" // *A Th* 26, 38; cf. 37: "slave of the living God," whereas Paul in his genuine letters prefers "slave of Christ" (Rom 1:1; 1 Cor 7:22).
- Both are circumspect about wealth and contain explicit or implied encouragement toward proper use of wealth: 1 Timothy 6:8–10, 17–19: "be generous, ready to share" // *A Th* 41: wealthy Tryphaena's beneficence toward Paul's ministry to the poor.
- Both presume enslaving human beings as normative: 1 Timothy 6:1–2; Titus 2:9–10 // *A Th* 10, 19, 36, 39–40. As part of the canonical New Testament, these passages concerning enslaved persons are among the texts that have a history of harm, having been used to justify the unjustifiable. See Smith, "Slavery in the Early Church"; Smith, "Paul and African American Biblical Interpretation"; Thurman, *Jesus and the Disinherited*, esp. ch. 1.

We encourage you to read the PE for yourself and look for points of agreement and contrast within them, with the *A Th*, and with Paul's seven genuine letters and the other letters attributed to Paul in the New Testament (the other Deutero-Pauline letters: Colossians, Ephesians, 2 Thessalonians). Our focus here is to introduce you to the *A Th* in relation to the PE.

While acknowledging the different genres — the PE are letters, the *A Th* is a narrative in the style of the Greek romances — the *A Th* and 1 Timothy nonetheless often diverge within agreements. The *A Th* redefines women's roles and salvation in contrast to the way 1 Timothy 2:8–15 does, arguably deliberately so. Both address concerns about the roles and social norms for women in the community and in relation to the outside world. And both articulate a concern for continuity in leadership by establishing a connection to Paul to legitimize their messages. However, while 1 Timothy and Titus restrict certain leadership roles to men (e.g., overseer), and 1

Timothy restricts women's roles, the *ATh* is an argument in narrative form for broader female roles and leadership. Although both accept as legitimate the leadership role of the male head of household (*paterfamilias*), as is clear from Onesiphoros in the *ATh* and 1 Timothy 3:4–5, the *ATh* has a sharper focus on leadership beyond the *paterfamilias*. The PE employs the image of the *paterfamilias*, implied in 1 Timothy 2:12 and more explicit in 1 Timothy 3:4–5 and Titus 2:3–5, as a way of establishing order and decorum in assembly.[11] The Pastor likely was influenced by a particular understanding of 1 Corinthians 11:1–12 that emphasized the culturally defined gender roles in vv. 1–10 and de-emphasized v. 11.[12] Thecla, in contrast, embeds herself in the Christian *paterfamilias*, placing herself under the care of God, explaining her freedom as an itinerant teacher. A revealing, stark contrast concerns the way the two works encapsulate their messages: In 1 Timothy 1:4, the gospel is called "God's household plan," whereas in the *ATh* God's word concerns "self-control and resurrection" (5).

Both texts are concerned with true and false teachings by which the authors construct or extend boundaries within the group and in relation to the outside world. Notably, 1 Timothy focuses on false teachings in relation to "teachers of the law" (1 Tim 1:7) that may relate to requiring "abstinence from foods" (1 Tim 4:3). It is unclear whether the latter refers solely to ascetic practices, as is sometimes assumed, or to not eating foods prohibited in the Hebrew Bible as a practice encouraged by "those from the circumcision" (cf. Titus 1:10: "Jewish Christians").[13] The three letters that comprise the PE contain

---

[11] The occurrence of "under control" (*hypotage*) in 1 Timothy 2:11 and 3:4 points toward reading 1 Timothy 2:11 as also concerning household management.

[12] Regarding 1 Corinthians 11:1–12, see Schüssler Fiorenza, *In Memory of Her*, 226–30; Collins, *First Corinthians*, 410–11; Blount, *Then the Whisper Put on Flesh*, ch. 5.

[13] Perkins notes that the reference to "purity" ("clean" in NAB) in Titus 1:15 "suggests that the commandments in question concerned purity or kosher regulations" ("Pastoral Epistles," 1434). There is no firm evidence for or against the possibility that the "teachers of the law" were Jewish. In addition, 1 Timothy placing together rejection of marriage and abstinence from foods is a rhetorical grouping that likely masks a more complex historical situation in which some Jesus adherents promoted an asceticism related to marriage while others — not necessarily of Jewish descent — adhered to Jewish food regulations to varying degrees (cf. Acts 15:29:

vague references to a variety of groups that the Pastor considers problematic. As Anna Solevåg notes, "These labels serve as invective, in order to categorize the opponent as 'other.'"[14] Although the *A Th* never mentions a circumcision faction or diet restrictions, ascetic practices are important to the narrative. It is interesting that there is no mention of meat or wine in the list of food in the tomb (*A Th* 25): "five loaves and vegetables and water [and salt]."

Both are interested in salvation and the path to salvation, which we address further below after reflecting on other points of tension.

Learning and Teaching: Instructions for Women in the Household of God

Let us first compare and contrast the *A Th* with the Pastor's teaching about women's roles and salvation in the famously controversial passage 1 Tim 2:8–15. This text addresses both "proper" conduct for women and salvation, specifically for married women within assembly (community gathering) in accordance with their place in the household:[15]

> [8] It is my wish, then, that in every place the men should pray, lifting up holy hands, without anger or argument. [9] Similarly, [too] women should adorn themselves with proper conduct, with modesty and self-control, not with braided hairstyles and gold adornments, or pearls, or expensive clothes, [10] but rather, as befits women who profess reverence for God, with good deeds. [11] A woman must receive instruction silently and under complete control. [12] I do not permit a woman to teach or to have authority over a man. She must be quiet. [13] For Adam was formed first, then Eve. [14] Further, Adam was not deceived, but the woman was deceived and transgressed. [15] But she will be saved through

---

"Abstain from meat sacrificed to idols, from blood, from meats of strangled animals, and from unlawful marriage"). We cannot assume that the Pastor represents accurately the opponents' viewpoints.

[14] Solevåg, *Birthing Salvation*, 90.

[15] See Solevåg, *Birthing Salvation*, esp. ch. 3. Her study examines 1 Timothy 2:15 in relation to childbearing discourse in the *Martyrdom of Perpetua and Felicitas* and the *Acts of Andrew*.

motherhood, provided women persevere in faith and love and holiness, with self-control.

Discussion of the passage is necessary to assist in comprehending what the Pastor is doing, specifically how the Pastor's linkage of women's roles and salvation contrasts with the *ATh*. Before we examine this link between salvation and the virtues tied to modesty ("self-control"), we draw your attention to other aspects of the Pastor's comments on women's roles pertaining to learning and teaching within the household, which culminate with the statement on salvation.

First, the Pastor states that a woman must receive instruction silently and "under control."[16] Thecla conforms to the Pastor's wishes regarding modesty insofar as she becomes silent after hearing Paul's message from her window. Although her silence would have been viewed as appropriately modest for a woman in Greco-Roman culture, her silence may also convey the shock she has undergone in hearing a message that has changed her life and its trajectory. (We discuss her silence further in chapter 5.) Inappropriate behavior for a woman in that culture, however, occurs when Thecla wanders about alone at night searching for Paul and when she rolls on the ground at the spot where Paul had taught (20). The latter, which was excised from the Coptic form of the Thecla story, would have been considered a lack of control (acratic behavior). The *ATh* was willing to include this acratic behavior through its strong connection to *An Ephesian Tale*, as noted in chapter 2. Thus, there is tension between the *ATh* and 1 Timothy 2:11 in the way the *ATh* narrates how Thecla learns from Paul in relation to the Pastor's instructions for women learning in the home, under control.

---

[16] "Silently" is sometimes rendered "quietly." For reasons against that reading, see Zamfir, "The Topos of Female Hiddenness," 75–87. The phrase at 1 Timothy 2:11, "under control" (*hypotage*) relates to 1 Timothy 3:4 regarding children "under control."

Second, the Pastor assumes that women will display modesty within the household, with the *paterfamilias* as head of household.[17] When Thecla refuses to marry Thamyris, she has rejected the model that the Pastor and her own mother find indispensable. Thecla's rejection of marriage and children is also a disconnect with the Greek romances. It is important to acknowledge, however, that the *ATh* is not hostile to marriage and children per se, as Onesiphoros represents an ascetic *paterfamilias* with wife and children. The Pastor's embrace of typical household management order makes control of women under the *paterfamilias* a cultural presupposition that the historical Paul also shared to some extent (1 Cor 7:2; 11:1–10; Rom 1:26), but Paul never connects *salvation* to women's subordination within the household in his genuine letters.[18] To be clear, Thecla's learning from Paul would not be a problem for the Pastor. However, Thecla's rejection of marriage and therefore also childbearing as a young woman clearly would not sit well with the Pastor (cf. 1 Tim 5:14). Since her role as Paul's student leads to her desire to be an apostolic teacher in her own right, we now turn to another way in which the *ATh* extends the bounds of household management.

Third, Thecla's teaching role in the *ATh* exhibits a strong disconnect with the Pastor's wishes. The Pastor, speaking on behalf of Paul himself and therefore assuming Paul's authority, insists, "I do not permit a woman to teach or to have authority over a man. She must be quiet" (1 Tim 2:12). The Pastor here refers to women teaching in the context of community assembly, although that link is

---

[17] Regarding the role of the *paterfamilias*—the husband, father, head of household, master of slaves—see the box in ch. 3 on patronage and Osiek and MacDonald, *A Woman's Place*, 18–26.

[18] Despite Galatians 3:28 and 1 Corinthians 11:11, Luke Timothy Johnson notes that the submission of women to men was the basic cultural assumption and was a view that Paul shared in 1 Corinthians 7:2, which mentions a "married woman" (*gyne hypandros*, literally "an under-a-man-woman"; *First and Second Letters to Timothy*, 207). In Titus 2:4–5, the Pastor advises that young women should be taught to be modest, pure, good home managers, and under the control of the husband. Regarding masculine exercise of control over self and others in the household, see Glancy, "Protocols of Masculinity"; D'Angelo, "'Knowing How to Preside over His Own Household.'"

not explicit.[19] Initially, Thecla appears to conform to this injunction; a careful reading of the *A Th* reveals that she teaches women (39), specifically a woman, Tryphaena, and then through her also the enslaved women in her household also come to believe, although the *A Th* nowhere has Thecla teach in the context of a Christian assembly. In the context of the PE, it is conceivable, for instance, that widows taught young women in a home,[20] as Titus 2:3-4 infers. However, the *A Th* ends with a statement that Thecla "enlightened many with the word of God." The verb "enlightened" undoubtedly alludes to teaching, and the adjective "many" is masculine plural in Greek (*pollous*) and includes both men and women. While Thecla's testimony to the governor (37) certainly foreshadows her enlightening many, only the final line of the story clarifies that Thecla extends the bounds of her teaching role beyond what the Pastor might approve. The *A Th* concludes with a strong suggestion that Thecla was, like Paul, an itinerant missionary. In contrast to some of the women in Paul's genuine letters (e.g., Prisca and Aquila in Rom 16:3; Junia and Andronicus in Rom 16:7), where women are often paired with a man, this inference about Thecla's apostolic teaching ministry says nothing about spousal or male partnership,[21] nor does the *A Th* identify the context in which Thecla teaches other than that it is in Tryphaena's home.

In an astute reading of the way the Pastor transfers women's idealized role in the household to the assembly, Korinna Zamfir summarizes this passage as follows:

> The respectable woman is inconspicuous, unassuming, disdainful of ostentatious adornment, modest, silent, submitted to male authority. She keeps her being and inner world hidden. Dress codes, silence and submission are chief means of this inconspicuousness. She remains in the private sphere abiding by traditional female roles.[22]

---

[19] Perkins, "Pastoral Epistles," 1434.

[20] See Thurston, "1 Timothy 5:3-16 and the Leadership of Women," 172.

[21] Cf. Philippians 4:2-3, where Euodia and Syntyche struggled at Paul's side in apostolic ministry.

[22] Zamfir, "The Topos of Female Hiddenness," 486.

Thecla in the *A Th* gradually sheds silence and submission to the extent that by the time the narrative ends, she is an itinerant apostolic teacher who has received Paul's blessing to "go, teach the word of God." When she is saved in the arena and asked to explain herself to the Antioch governor, the text places Thecla squarely in the public sphere and draws attention to her testimony, which is decidedly at odds with the Pastor's assessment of hiddenness as ideal for women.

Before we turn to how the Pastor links gender norms to salvation, we wish to pause for a moment to acknowledge the harm that 1 Timothy 2:8–15 has caused historically and still causes to this day. It is a "proof text" that has been used throughout the history of Western Christianity and is sometimes still used today in sexist ways. The harm has most directly affected women and includes reinforcing ideologies of gender. Clarice Martin explains,

> Patriarchy, which presupposes that males alone are best and most fully represent the interest, gifts, and potential of both women and men in church and society, is a jagged blade: it not only "cuts" by distorting the human construction of reality in which men and women together are both equally and fully created in the image of God (Gen 1:26–31), it "cuts" and devastates by sanctifying the dominion of some members of the human family over others—a tradition and social practice African Americans rejected outright in the evil institution of American slavery (which legitimated the dominion of white Americans over black Americans).[23]

Luke Timothy Johnson notes ways in which features of this text are problematic as normative for today, including that the teaching is based on the Pastor's individual authority ("I do not permit") and on a common problematic reading of Genesis 3.[24] The *A Th* provides an early Christian counternarrative that challenges the Pastor's proscriptions.

---

[23] Martin, *True to Our Native Land*, 423.

[24] Johnson, *First and Second Timothy*, 211. For critical rereadings of Genesis 3, see Hayes, *Forged in A Fiery Furnace*, 144–47; Trible, *God and the Rhetoric of Sexuality*, ch. 4.

Up to this point, we have compared and contrasted learning and teaching in the *A Th* with the Pastor's views on married women in the home in 1 Timothy 2:8–15. We now turn to how the Pastor connects salvation with culturally defined female roles in relation to marriage.

Salvation: Are Women Saved Differently from Men?

The most interesting and important point of tension between the *A Th* and the PE concerns salvation. The Pastor and the *A Th* have broad agreement that salvation is for all (1 Tim 2:4, 6; Titus 2:11; cf. 1 Tim 1:15; 6:13 // *A Th* 17), and they even startlingly leave open the possibility of salvation for those who are not Christian (1 Tim 4:10; *A Th* 28–29). The Pastor, however, is also concerned that his congregation conform to women's specific roles in teaching and learning and managing a home that were common norms found in the surrounding Greco-Roman culture. The Pastor states, "But she will be saved through motherhood, provided women persevere in faith and agapic love and holiness, with modesty" (1 Tim 2:15). The sentence suggests that women are saved through motherhood, often translated as "childbearing," within marriage, and then links the salvation to maintaining social honor and modesty in the home, *distinct from how men are saved*. We will devote the rest of the chapter to this theological point.

Had the Pastor linked salvation only with faith, agapic love, and holiness, there would be little to contrast with Thecla. As we noted above, the *A Th* and 1 Timothy have a broad agreement that salvation is for everyone. At issue is that he links salvation here to the birth-giving role and then to virtues—not those virtues of faith and agapic love on their own—that he specifically ties to female modesty, which in Greco-Roman culture was considered a virtue particularly associated with married women. In other words, the Pastor here writes directives to his community about women's decorum in assembly and then uses language of salvation and theological virtues in gender-exclusive ways in order to persuade his audience to comply with his culturally specific preference. The *A Th* never associates salvation with female modesty.

Box 4: Readings of 1 Timothy 2:15 on Women's Salvation

Scholars have a variety of ways of understanding the Pastor's statement in v. 15 linking female salvation to childbearing and to "faith, agapic love, and holiness, with modesty." Commentaries on 1 Timothy provide the basic contours of the debate, and we refer you to those works. Particularly helpful are the following overviews: Solevåg, *Birthing Salvation: Gender and Class in Early Christian Childbearing Discourse*, 87–96; Porter, "What Does It Mean to be 'Saved by Childbirth' (1 Tim 2:15)?"

Some commentators argue for a nontheological understanding in which the text refers, for instance, to women being rescued from harm in childbirth. Most commentators assume that the Pastor is making a theological statement about salvation and that he aims the discourse of the verse at a group of opponents, often thought to have problematic ascetic views. In this reading, the Pastor promotes having children here and also in 1 Timothy 5:14 as a response to those who "forbid marriage" (1 Tim 4:3). It is common to link this passage directly with cultural norms of the time, as Bassler explains: "Cultural norms control the ethical perspective throughout these letters, making it sometimes difficult to determine which admonitions were given because they are ethical commonplace, and which reflect concrete problems within the community."[25] Reconstructions of the precise historical context for 1 Timothy 2:15 in relation to opponents, though often interesting, involve piecing together disparate clues in the PE that result in a conjectural opponent. Since the Pastor applies a variety of labels that "serve as invective to categorize the opponent as 'other,'" Solevåg wisely cautions against assuming that we have access to the precise views of the opponents.[26] In her reading of the PE as a whole, the Pastor links salvation to proper household

---

[25] Bassler, *1 Timothy, 2 Timothy, Titus*, 63.
[26] Solevåg, *Birthing Salvation*, 90.

conduct: "Salvation is dependent on childbearing and right child-rearing—the first being the responsibility of the mother, the second of both the mother *and* the kyriarchal father."[27] Further, the Pastor singles out women in 1 Timothy 2:13-15 through a reading of Genesis 3 in which childbearing is both a punishment for transgression and also part of redemption. Her reading is somewhat similar to that of Raymond Collins, who sees the Pastor engaging in a midrash (a type of Jewish interpretation) on the creation story.[28] Solevåg's reading emphasizes the Pastor's gender ideology, which sharply distinguishes male and female roles.

The Pastor in 1 Timothy 2:15 places rhetorical pressure on the community to behave in ways that he considers appropriate to God's household plan of salvation, and in that plan young women submit to marriage and childbearing. Men also submit to God's household plan, but they do so as head of household (*paterfamilias*), with everyone in the home in subordinate roles. The pastor never explicitly singles out males as having a unique path to salvation within the household in contrast to the pressure applied to young women in vv. 13-15. Collins rightly cautions that letters are compositions "whose essential import relates immediately and directly only to the situation that dictated their composition."[29]

The Pastor consistently emphasizes the importance of marriage and childbearing for women, as is the case in 1 Timothy 5:14 regarding young widows: "So I would like younger widows to marry, have children, and manage a home, so as to give the adversary no pretext for maligning us."[30] In that passage, the Pastor links women's proper roles in the home, including managing the home, to concern for how those outside the movement view it. The

---

[27] Solevåg, *Birthing Salvation*, 133.

[28] Collins, *1 & 2 Timothy and Titus*, 74-75.

[29] Collins, *1 & 2 Timothy and Titus*, 75.

[30] For a deeper engagement of 1 Timothy 5 and the *ATh*, see MacDonald, *Early Christian Women*, 154-82; Bassler, "A Fresh Look at 1 Tim 5:3-16."

Pastor presumably fears that failure to conform to these culturally defined gender norms will result in problems for the community in and out of assembly. Some scholars see the Pastor countering the teachings of the anonymous "some" (1 Tim 1:3-7: teachers of the law) who forbid marriage (4:3). As Perkins notes, the false teachers are described as upsetting whole households (Titus 1:11).[31] It is only in 1 Timothy 2:15, however, that he goes so far as to link these gender norms to salvation, something that Paul never does in his genuine letters and is unique in the Christian canon.

Clearly, baptism and faith are the centers of salvation in the *ATh*, and salvation derives from actions of God and Jesus to deliver in the present and the future (17, 37-38). The *ATh* rejects the notion that women are saved by having children. In the Iconium portion, the message of salvation through childbearing is presented as *oppositional* to Paul's teaching on purity in the beatitudes (5-6): "Blessed are those who keep the flesh undefiled," and again, "Blessed are those who have wives as though they did not," and again, "Blessed are the bodies of virgins." If there is any doubt as to how these teachings were interpreted by the audience, Demas and Hermogenes clarify, "Who this man is we do not know. But he would deprive young men of wives and young women of husbands" (12).

Box 5: Demas and Hermogenes and 1 Timothy 2:15

> Scholars consistently connect Demas and Hermogenes to the teachings of the PE. When we are first introduced to Demas and Hermogenes, we learn that they are hypocrites (literally "two-faced"), using similar language for false teachers as 1 Timothy. In the *ATh*, while talking to Thamyris, they suggest that they will teach "that what [Paul] calls resurrection has

---

[31] Perkins, "Pastoral Epistles," 1434. See also Titus 2:3-5 regarding women. The Pastor expresses concern for the views of outsiders in 1 Timothy 3:7 (an administrative overseer must have a good reputation among outsiders) and 6:1 (concern that improper behavior of the enslaved person could result in the teachings being defamed). See Solevåg, *Birthing Salvation*, 89-91, for a balanced overview and critique of these reconstructions.

already happened when we have children" (14). Because they talk about having children as a way of fulfilling the resurrection, they are associated with 1 Tim 2:15.

Problematically Demas and Hermogenes do not appear together in the PE, nor are they described as false teachers. Rather, they both have left Paul, and Demas is "enamored of the present world" (2 Tim 4:9–10—see the grid above). In the PE, it is Hymenaeus and Philetus, in 2 Timothy 2:17–18, who are described as having left the faith because they are teaching that the resurrection "has already taken place," and it is the Pastor who connects childbirth to salvation, not resurrection. To resolve these inconsistencies, den Dulk suggests that we view Demas and Hermogenes as composite figures for all of the opponents in 2 Timothy. Both the *ATh* and 2 Timothy 2:17–18 reject the idea that "the resurrection has already happened," and both connect the teaching with false teachers.[32]

This is yet another example of *ATh* agreeing with 2 Timothy while disagreeing with 1 Timothy. Demas and Hermogenes are hypocrites and liars, both in what they say (teaching that there is a connection between resurrection and having children) and what they do (lie, endanger Paul—the true teacher—and eat a luxurious meal, embracing "the present world"). This is a fascinating moment in the *ATh* (13–14): Demas, Hermogenes, and Thamyris sit over a luxurious meal, strategize how to get Paul executed, and promulgate their own message connecting childbirth with resurrection.

In addition to the direct teaching of Paul, the *ATh* also counters the teaching that women are saved through childbirth in the depiction of the female characters, particularly Thecla herself and Falconilla, neither of whom marry. Moreover, the surrogate mother, Tryphaena, lost her child, Falconilla, before Thecla had taught her about the faith. Thecla mediates Falconilla's transference to the place

---

[32] Den Dulk, "I Permit No Woman to Teach," 196.

of the righteous. Later, Tryphaena comes to believe through witnessing the miracles in the arena (39). The Thecla narrative provides several examples of women who are saved, none of them through childbirth.

Finally, there is Thecla herself pursuing salvation. She is clearly driven, after hearing the teachings of Paul, to commit to a life of purity, receive baptism, and spread the message that Paul, the moral teacher and mediator of God's word, infused in her. The *ATh* is a narrative in which Thecla is saved multiple times in the sense of rescue from danger: by divine intervention through an earthquake; by her maternal patron Tryphaena, who takes her into her home; by the crowd of protesting women who provide support and throw oils and herbs in the arena; and finally when Tryphaena faints to halt Thecla's final near-martyrdom. Three times the *ATh* articulates a message about ultimate or theological salvation (17, 37–38). None of the devices that save Thecla throughout the narrative—whether rescue from danger or statements on ultimate theological salvation—have to do with childbearing or with faith, agapic love, and holiness qualified by modest behavior particular to women. Rather, the three theological statements on salvation in the *ATh* connect salvation directly with God and Christ without gender qualifications:

> 17: a God . . . who desires the salvation of human beings.

> 37: I believe in His Son, in whom God is well pleased. On account of whom not one of the beasts touched me. For He alone is the pillar of salvation and the foundation of eternal life.

> 38: He will clothe me with salvation on the Day of Judgment.

God saves human beings without gender qualification in the *ATh*, as is also the case in 1 Timothy 1:15; 2:3-6 and Titus 2:11, but in contrast to 1 Timothy 2:15.

Conclusion

The Pastor's advocacy for particular women's roles and decorum in assembly devolves in 1 Timothy 2:15 into an attempt to bolster his views through appealing to married women's roles in the home as related to salvation. In making directives about social norms for the community gathering, which was done in homes, the Pastor distinguishes between proper behavior for men and women and ties female behavior and placement in the household with her salvation, childbearing, and modesty. The Pastor makes an explicit theological statement that women are saved through childbearing and their ongoing proper behavior. In contrast, the *ATh* in narrative form contains an implicit argument against tying women's salvation to modest behavior as a mother bearing children. Most of Thecla's actions take place outside of the household and eventually lead to her teaching and traveling, like Paul, which stands in tension with the Pastor's directives.

Both texts, in their way, are describing an idealized image of a woman. The PE argues that young women should be properly embedded in the *paterfamilias*—married, silent, unassuming, having children, all with modesty. By contrast, Thecla is never in the home with a *paterfamilias*; she is either in her mother's home or Tryphaena's, and ultimately the narrative places her within the household of God, who is her only *paterfamilias*. Additionally, the *ATh* presents an image of an elite young woman coming to the Christian faith, which was atypical for most women in the Greco-Roman world, most of whom were not elite. And while there is an openness to salvation for all people in both texts, there are clear tensions between 1 Timothy 2:15 and the *ATh* regarding salvation that are particular to married women. The many tensions implicit between the Thecla narrative and 1 Timothy point to the conclusion that the *ATh* was in part a corrective to problematic aspects of 1 Timothy, aimed at women's roles and salvation. Presenting the two side by side illustrates these deep tensions and clarifies how 1 Timothy 2:15 is theologically controversial.

The *ATh* contains several intriguing connections with 2 Timothy in themes, names, and locations that point to a more positive perspective on that letter in contrast to the prominent tensions with 1 Timothy. It is intriguing that even the plot of the *ATh* is an encapsulation of 2 Timothy 3:10–11 and especially of 2 Timothy

4:16–18 but with Thecla in place of Paul: "At my first defense no one appeared on my behalf, but everyone deserted me. May it not be held against them! But the Lord stood by me and gave me strength so that through me the proclamation might be completed and all the Gentiles might hear it. And I was rescued from the lion's mouth. The Lord will rescue me" (2 Tim 4:16–18).

We leave many questions for you to contemplate: What messages do you hear regarding gender in the Thecla text? How might we appropriate the messages in these ancient texts in responsible ways? Our hope is that we have helped frame the conversation and deepened engagement with both texts.

The next chapter is a series of questions and responses. Some of the questions continue discussions we started in these first four chapters, while in others we introduce entirely new ideas in anticipation of additional questions you may have developed while reading.

Chapter 5

Questions and Responses

This chapter addresses questions we often hear from students and other groups when we introduce them to the *A Th*. We refer to "responses" deliberately because we recognize that there are many ways of reading and responding to a text. Our hope here is to expand your understanding of the story while also providing more information about the historical context, connections to Greek romances and early Christian texts, and our thoughts on the theology and spirituality of the *A Th*. We hope this inspires you to continue investigating the story.

Questions and Responses: Socio-historical and Literary
How do you understand the physical description of Paul (3)?

The description of Paul tells the audience something about his character in relation to physical beauty and moral goodness, which were often related in the Greek romances. The view that a person's body revealed the person's moral character, called physiognomy, was a common cultural assumption in the Greco-Roman world. Writing many decades after Paul's life, the author of the *A Th* would have had no idea what the historical Paul looked like, but the text implies that views on the matter circulated, and there are ancient Christian artistic depictions of Paul from the catacombs. The author likely considered Titus to have known Paul personally, and the text states that Titus described Paul for Onesiphoros.

Titus describes Paul to Onesiphoros as follows: "A small man in size, bald in the head, curved in his legs, healthy, with a unibrow, with somewhat of a long nose, full of goodwill. For sometimes he appeared like a man, at other times he had the face of an angel" (3).

Most of these physical characteristics were not negative in that culture: A similar description of the nose, bowed or curved legs, and unibrow (eyebrows that meet) are also applied to Heracles.[1] But the ancient views are not univocal. For Galen, crooked legs are listed among negatives.[2] Views positive or negative about physical features are culturally dependent. Despite Galen's position, the description of Paul includes some physical aspects as a sign that Paul was healthy. The final two attributes in particular indicate that Paul's physical features reveal his moral goodness. His angelic face stands in relation to Thecla's vision of the Lord "sitting like Paul" (21), which associates Paul and Jesus with revelatory teaching. The Greek romances commonly comment on the beauty of the heroine's face (e.g., *Call* 2.2; 6.7; *DC* 1.24).

The feature that is most difficult to explain alongside the positive physical attributes is baldness. It may be that the author was relying on depictions of Paul as somewhat bald that survive in the catacombs and/or in the reference in Acts 18:18 that he shaved his hair as part of a vow.[3] Since some ancient writers (Aristotle, Seneca, Galen) associated baldness with a masculine lack of self-control or immoderate excess,[4] Paul's baldness for some in the Greco-Roman world would have been in tension with his message of self-control in the beatitudes. That tension accounts for the alteration in the Armenian translation, which gives Paul curly hair. The tension is perhaps similar to Thecla's embrace of Paul's message of self-control and her rolling on the spot where Paul had taught (20): Both were part of a received tradition, one derived from the catacombs and/or Acts 18:18, the other from *An Ephesian Tale*.

Some interpreters understand Paul's description as not entirely positive, including Jan Bremmer and Monika Betz. These scholars plausibly suggest that the ambivalent mixture of positive and negative physical attributes may be a way to distance the narrative

---

[1] Malherbe, "A Physical Description of Paul," 174–75.

[2] Galen, *On Temperaments* 2.6, 1.625–6k.

[3] Malherbe, "A Physical Description of Paul," 175.

[4] Aristotle, *On the Generation of Animals* 5.3 734b; Seneca, *Epistulae Morales* 95.16–21; Galen, *On Temperaments* 2.6, 1.625–6k.

from the claim that Thecla was in love with Paul romantically. Thecla, rather, falls in love with the gospel and is attracted to Paul as mediator of the message. A greater emphasis is placed on Thecla hearing Paul. Paul's physical description is to some extent the antitype of the beautiful romantic lover of the Greek romances, particularly in comparison to the extensive praise of male beauty in the Greek romances, as is the case with Daphnis's beautiful body (*DC* 1.3, 13–16). Thecla ridding herself of her mirror to visit Paul in prison is an additional relativization of beauty, as a mirror was associated with concern for female beauty.[5] An additional consideration: Depending on how one reads the Antioch scene in which Alexander grabs at Thecla (26), Paul's physical imperfection here may foreshadow his ethically compromised disavowal of Thecla when Alexander inquires about having her.

Further reading: Malherbe, "A Physical Description of Paul"; Betz, "Die Betörenden Worte des fremden Mannes"; Bremmer, *Maidens, Magic and Martyrs in Early Christianity*, 151–52; Vander Stichele and Penner, *Contextualizing Gender*, 44–50, 63–81; Callon, *Reading Bodies: Physiognomy as a Strategy of Persuasion in Early Christian Discourse*; Holmes, "Marked Bodies: Gender, Race, Class, Age, Disability, and Disease"; Malina and Neyrey, *Portraits of Paul: An Archaeology of Ancient Personality*, 146.

Is Paul depicted entirely positively or somewhat negatively in the ATh?

Scholars are divided on how the *ATh* depicts Paul. In general, feminist scholars tend to be more open to seeing Paul as being depicted negatively to some extent, particularly regarding his behavior (what he does and does not do) and words (what he says and does not say) in the scene in which Alexander grabs at Thecla (26). In our analysis in chapter 3, we acknowledged that some scholars understand Paul even in that scene as being depicted positively because he had previously (25) warned Thecla about another trial, and therefore his demurral of her baptism is

---

[5] Aubin, "Reversing Romance," 271; McLarty, *Thecla's Devotion*, 170.

understood in the context of her completing the period of initiation and testing prior to baptism. Paul will eventually support Thecla's apostolic teaching ministry (41), although he is never the agent of her baptism.[6] There we also noted that some in a Greco-Roman audience would likely have reacted negatively to Paul's response to Alexander since the heroine Thecla had no one to protect her from the powerful man's advances. Here we wish to broaden the discussion to include the *A Th* within the *Acts of Paul* and to think about the *A Th* apart from that work.

When the *A Th* is read in the context of the *AP*, where Paul is the hero, there is some additional pressure to understand the depiction of Paul as entirely positive. Even within the *A Th* itself, Paul often is depicted very positively as teacher and mediator. However, we have suggested that the physical description of Paul (3) can be read as not entirely positive and as a deliberate contrast to the depiction of the male hero in the Greek romances. Moreover, if one thinks about the *A Th* as circulating apart from the *AP* originally, as many scholars have proposed,[7] the differences between the *A Th* and the *AP* become more prominent, and one can see that a not entirely positive depiction of Paul in the *A Th* is a distinct possibility. On the tensions between the *A Th* and the larger *AP*, see the discussion below.

Another consideration concerns the complicated relationship between the *A Th* and the Pastoral Epistles examined in chapter 4. If the *A Th* looks more favorably on 2 Timothy than on 1 Timothy, both of which were composed in Paul's name, then a general embrace of Paul coupled with a hesitancy makes sense.

In sum, we favor a reading of the *A Th* that notes a combination of a fervent embrace of Paul as teacher and divine mediator and also a hesitancy about him that reflects our analysis of two key ambiguous texts, Paul's physical description (3) and his inaction during Alexander's assault (26). An understanding of those texts as

---

[6] For further discussion, see Edsall, "(Not) Baptizing Thecla."

[7] In particular, Esch-Wermeling, *Thekla-Paulusschülerin*, 205–6, 221–32. There is some disjointedness between the Iconium section and the Antioch section. See Aymer, "Hailstorms and Fireballs." See also Christine Thomas's discussion of "open text" in "Stories Without Texts and Without Authors," 289–90.

reflecting a mixed depiction of Paul coheres with the original existence of the *ATh* apart from the *AP* and with the complicated relationship the *ATh* seems to have with 2 Timothy (positive) and 1 Timothy (negative about the Pastor's views in 1 Tim 2:8-15). Nonetheless, the depiction of Paul in the *ATh* can be and often is read as thoroughly positive. This debate is an opportunity for you to read the text and decide how you think the *ATh* portrays him.

What is the significance of the beatitudes — the list of blessings — in ATh 5-6?

We highlight three ways to view Paul's beatitudes in the *ATh*: The beatitudes center the main teachings of the story, they play an important role in the narrative as a foreshadowing literary device, and they have obvious connections to beatitudes in other Christian writings.

Presented as coming directly from Paul, the beatitudes are the authoritative teachings that the implied author highlights regarding asceticism and salvation, which are framed as a message about self-control and resurrection (5). Particularly important is leaving the world, which the text highlights by restating the idea in different words. Also significant, there is no gender differentiation in these beatitudes. Both Onesiphoros and Thecla leave the world. It may seem strange at first that resurrection is not explicitly mentioned in the beatitudes. However, references to inheriting God, resting with God, judging angels, and being in the light probably refer to resurrection.[8]

It was common in antiquity for stories to include a summary or encapsulation, sometimes in several locations.[9] Summaries recur in the Greek romances (*ET* 1.6; 3.3; *Call* 5.1; 8.1, 7-8).[10] In the *ATh*, the beatitudes foreshadow what will happen in the story during Thecla's period of initiation and travails.[11] Thecla embodies the

---

[8] McLarty, *Thecla's Devotion*, 200.

[9] For the summaries in Mark's Gospel, see Tolbert, "Mark," 352-53.

[10] The oracle in *ET* 1.6 foreshadows what is to come.

[11] Aubin refers to "narrative premonition" ("Reversing Romance," 263). See also McLarty, *Thecla's Devotion*, 100-101, 201, who notes that "Thecla's prayer on

teachings of the beatitudes in the narrative in the following specific ways:

- she keeps the flesh undefiled
- renounces the world
- displays awe of the sayings of God
- receives the wisdom of Jesus Christ and therefore calls God "Father" (24)
- preserves baptism (34)
- possesses the insight of Jesus Christ and therefore is illuminated (42)
- is rewarded for her purity

The beatitudes bracket the entire narrative: They open the story with Paul teaching in Onesiphoros's house, and the story closes with Thecla's prayer in the same place.

The beatitudes in the *ATh* contain obvious connections to the beatitudes in Matthew 5:3–12 and Luke 6:20–23, with common themes of mercy and comforting. The first beatitude of section 6 regarding consolation derives from Matthew 5:4, but the *ATh* transforms the first part from "Blessed are those who mourn" to "Blessed are those who are in awe of the sayings of God," which fits more closely Thecla's actions in the story. Since consolation is important to the Greek romance genre, the *ATh* retains that part of the beatitude but transforms the other part in relation to Thecla's awe over Paul's teachings. Mourning would be less appropriate to the story. This transformation is a clear indication that these beatitudes frame the narrative.

The beatitudes also find parallels in Paul's letters, as is the case with Rom 12:9–21.[12] Another change occurs in *ATh* 6 with "Blessed are the merciful, for they will be shown mercy and they will not see the harsh Day of Judgment," which derives from Matthew 5:7: "Blessed are the merciful for they will be shown mercy." The *ATh* adds the last clause about avoidance of judgment — another way in

---

her return to Onesiphoros' house is significant for its economical summary of the episodes of the plot" (100).

[12] Regarding application of beatitudes to today, see Pfeil, "A Spirituality of White Nonviolent Resistance," esp. 155–57.

which the *ATh* consoles the audience and directs them to a course of action, here to exercise mercy.

What do you make of the beatitude (5) "Blessed are those who had wives as though they did not"?

This beatitude stands firmly within a stream of thinking that Paul addresses in 1 Corinthians 7:1–7 in which some married couples in the Corinthian community were refraining from sexual intercourse. Paul responds to a question about sex within marriage and advises in vv. 5–6: "Do not deprive each other, except by mutual consent for a time, to be free for prayer, but then return to one another, so that Satan may not tempt you through your lack of self-control. This I say by way of concession, however, not as a command." Some people in Corinth seem to have understood Paul's views on the urgency of the return of Christ and his preference for celibacy as indicating that married couples should no longer have sexual intercourse.

This beatitude indicates that Paul's mixed messages regarding self-control and the urgency of Christ's return were affecting people's views even in the late second century. This beatitude in the *ATh* reflects an openness to celibacy within marriage, though whether permanently or for set periods the text does not elaborate. Chaste marriages recur in the Apocryphal Acts of the Apostles[13] and are known in the Syriac Christian tradition of *qadishe,* a second rank of Syrian ascetics, couples who live together in chastity. Thus, the *ATh* stands within a line of interpretation of 1 Corinthians 7 while acknowledging through the character Onesiphoros that family life is also an option. Whether Onesiphoros and his wife Lectra, who have two children, were abstaining from sexual intercourse upon entering the Christ movement is not explicitly stated in the narrative.

---

[13] See Konstan, "Acts of Love."

What do you make of the spider imagery (9) that Thecla's mother uses to describe to Thamyris Thecla's fixation on Paul?

This imagery is interesting and has been subject to a variety of interpretations. It is debated whether the text compares Thecla or Paul to a spider. This simile is part of Theocleia's extended complaint about Paul and the effects Paul is having on the previously properly behaved Thecla. Theocleia says to Thamyris (9), "And *still* my daughter, like a spider at the window imprisoned by his words, is controlled by a new lust and a gravely powerful passion. For she observes closely the words spoken by him and the young woman is conquered." The forthcoming critical edition reads: "My daughter also, immobilized by his words as a spider to the window."

It is commonly observed that the original audience may have heard an allusion to the famous story of Arachne in the background (the Greek word for spider is *arachne*). In that story, Arachne is particularly gifted in the traditional women's work of weaving, but she oversteps her human limitations by considering her weaving to be superior to Athena's. Arachne's pride and inordinate desire results in her death, and she is transformed into a spider. Reading Theocleia's words with the Arachne story as background has merit, as this section of the *ATh* depicts Thecla undergoing a metamorphosis from a modest daughter betrothed to Thamyris to (from Theocleia's perspective) someone caught up in a predatory stranger's harmful message about chastity. On the one hand, her mother considers Thecla imprisoned or immobilized by Paul at the window and is under his control, in which case Paul is likened to a spider and Thecla to his ensnared prey. On the other hand, spiders can themselves be bound, and the Arachne story can be understood as alluding to egregious desire.

Jeremy Hultin observes that Thecla's desire is "ruinous both to her own family (witness her mother's horror) and to the stability of society."[14] Pervo focuses on the phrase "trapped in her window by the web of his message" (his translation) and understands the

---

[14] Hultin, "A New Web for Arachne," 216–17. For other readings of this text, see McLarty, *Thecla's Devotion*, 181; Spittler, *Animals in the Apocryphal Acts*, 164.

metaphor to refer to Paul: "The image of Paul as a spider feminizes him, since spiders weave, a primary activity of women."[15] It may be that the referent for the simile — whether the spider is Paul or Thecla — is deliberately ambiguous. The simile is at any rate part of Theocleia's depiction of Paul as a stranger and magician (8) who has cast a spell on her daughter, causing her immobilization.

What is the significance of Thecla remaining silent for a prolonged period of time?

Scholars have a variety of responses to this difficult question. Here we present a few possibilities: Thecla's silence can be seen as an example of endurance, a form of lovesickness, and/or as a trickster response to the social expectation of hiddenness and silence.

McLarty emphasizes that Thecla's silence is an achievement related to her endurance: "It is only when she has endured all her trials that she is transformed from suffering object to speaking subject, exhibiting a masculine ability to use persuasive rhetoric in the theatre's public setting in deliberate contrast to her silence in court."[16] Endurance is brought up explicitly twice in the *ATh*, in sections 21 and 25, but is also a leitmotif in the beatitudes when Paul emphasizes self-control and says, "Blessed are those who keep the flesh undefiled" (5). Endurance was a particularly masculine virtue in antiquity that is emphasized in martyrdom texts such as 4 Maccabees and in the Greek romances. For Hylen, Thecla's silence in the first part of the story emphasizes the virtue of modesty appropriate to women, while Thecla's bold speaking in Antioch does not detract from her already established virtue.[17]

Speechlessness and silence are connected to lovesickness, modesty, and self-control in the Greek romances, among other usages. Daphnis becomes quiet and doesn't eat on account of his love for Chloe (*DC* 1.17–18). Callirhoe's speechlessness (*Call* 1.1) is

---

[15] Pervo, *The Acts of Paul*, 110–12.

[16] McLarty, *Thecla's Devotion*, 112.

[17] Hylen, *Modest Apostle*, 75–78. See also Kraemer's discussion of Thecla's silence in *Unreliable Witnesses*, 140–41.

seen by others as an expression of modesty even though it is a deliberate refusal to speak. Callirhoe's silence and modesty are juxtaposed (*Call* 6.7), while Mithridates directly connects Chaereas's silence with self-control (*Call* 4.3). Another (not incompatible) consideration: Thecla is undergoing a period of silence while in a phase of discipleship or initiation in which she follows the teachings of God's revelatory messenger, Paul.[18] Thecla's silence, then, may have had multiple compatible functions and resonances for the original audience: Silence is a sign of modesty appropriate to women and for an initiate; her silence is also related to her achievement of endurance of many trials through a masculine self-discipline (self-control).

An entirely different explanation of Thecla's silence arises when comparing her silence with stories of women who seemingly follow a rule but do so as a trickster for some greater good, such as personal safety or the security of a child. This trickster archetype is found in the Bible and Greek literature, including the romances, and is common in African American literature, with antecedents in the period of enslavement. Brer Rabbit is an archetypal trickster in a context of unequal power dynamics. In some forms of this archetype, the women do not trick solely to be deceptive, although that archetype is also available. Rather, they work within social norms in unexpected ways to achieve a desired outcome. Moses's mother is an example. She follows Pharaoh's edict, "Throw into the river every boy that is born to the Hebrews" (Exod 1:22), but she does so in a trickster way by putting the baby in a basket first. In this way, she subverts and follows the unjust edict simultaneously.

Applying this archetype to Thecla's silence, Thecla is silent, as the Pastor (1 Tim 2:11–12) indicates is appropriate for women, but she does not accept the implied subordination that the Pastor requires. Her silence conforms to expectations of female modesty while also allowing her to maintain a period of Christian discipleship toward a greater good, her baptism. Her silence angers her mother and Thamyris but is technically not offensive in itself. It

---

[18] See Johnson, *Among the Gentiles*, 82. In relation to the *ATh*, see esp. ch. 5–6 and pp. 159–64.

is fun to play with the text in this regard because there are other examples of a paradox of power in which those who seem to have the power, especially Thamyris and Alexander, become powerless in the course of the narrative.

Something similar happens with the female characters in the Greek romances: Women are not entirely truthful when confronted by people who might be dangerous or placed in comparable difficult situations. When she becomes enslaved, Callirhoe has to be circumspect about herself with the people she meets. She is not always truthful with Dionysius in her efforts to return to Habrocomes. Also, to save her baby, she conceals that Habrocomes, not Dionysius, is the father (*Call* 2.11). In her prayer to Aphrodite (*Call* 3.2), Callirhoe asks the goddess to "allow me to keep my strategy secret." Trickster behavior in the Greek romances is particularly important for the heroine maintaining chastity. In *ET* 5.7, Antheia pretends to have the divine disease, what we now call epilepsy, to avoid being a prostitute. At *ET* 5.14, when Antheia and Habrocomes finally reunite, she tells him that she remained pure and employed every stratagem of chastity to do so.

Further reading on the trickster archetype: Niditch, *Underdogs and Tricksters: A Prelude to Biblical Folklore*; Camp, "Wise and Strange: An Interpretation of the Female Imagery in Proverbs in Light of Trickster Mythology"; Chan, "The Ultimate Trickster in the Story of Tamar from a Feminist Perspective"; Jackson, "Lot's Daughters and Tamar as Tricksters and the Patriarchal Narratives as Feminist Theology"; Marshall, "Anansi, Eshu, and Legba: Slave Resistance and the West African Trickster"; Marshall, "'Nothing but Pleasant Memories of the Discipline of Slavery': The Trickster and the Dynamics of Racial Representation."

Why does the ATh *announce that Thamyris was found dead at the end of the story, and how might that announcement relate to the language of control and ownership of women in the narrative?*

The text uses language of control and ownership to portray Thamyris's relationship to Thecla. The narrator describes Thamyris as frightened by Thecla's "disturbed passion" (10) and Thecla as

103

belonging to him (10). The story depicts him spying on Paul, whom he incorrectly thinks is Thecla's lover (11), attempting to reacquire her "out of love" for her (13), and wandering the streets looking for her (19). He clearly wants to reclaim Thecla.

While there is much to explore regarding violence against women as a problem in relation to Alexander's quest for vengeance and the restoration of his honor, her mother's call for her execution through burning, and the gratuitous violence against Thecla's body, here we discuss a plausible reason for the death announcement: Thamyris can be perceived as posing a potential threat to Thecla (in different ways for ancient and modern audiences).

In the final paragraph of the *ATh* (43), the narrator states that Thamyris was found dead. He was last referred to in the story in paragraphs 19 (looking for Thecla) and 26 (the governor questions Thecla about her disobedience of Iconian law in her refusal to marry Thamyris), which is to say that Thamyris is a main character in the first half of the *ATh* but is absent from the second half until we are informed about his demise. His death resolves something, but it is not clear what is being resolved. We should probably be mindful that the *ATh* tells us very little about Thecla and even less about Thamyris. The narrative never tells us their respective ages. It is likely that Thecla is a teenager; Thamyris could be a few years older than Thecla, though he might be much older. With so much information lacking, we are left to speculate about motives for the announcement of Thamyris's death.

In the Greco-Roman literary context, Thamyris's actions in the first half of the narrative are similar to the jilted suitors of the Greek romances, while the reference to him as found dead in the final paragraph is an aspect of storytelling in which the narrator ties up the plot's loose ends, also a feature of the Greek romances. In the final paragraph of *An Ephesian Tale*, for instance, the narrator states that the parents of the main characters died of old age and despair. From a literary perspective, then, the announcement of Thamyris's death is not entirely surprising.

In socio-historical context, the language about Thamyris and his behavior relate to gendered social norms rooted in values of honor and shame and culturally specific betrothal and marriage customs. We explore this matter to some extent in the section below on the question "What motivates Thecla's mother's deep anger at her daughter's refusal to marry Thamyris?" (see pp. 113–15) where we note that the *ATh* is silent about the gift exchange between the families in the betrothal process. Since the repayment of gift exchanges could sometimes take years,[19] the statement about Thamyris's demise would have brought closure to the original audience regarding questions they may have had about the potential betrothal debt.[20] Marriage abduction, which was not unknown in the Greco-Roman world and was a key part of one of the founding myths of the Roman people (the abduction of the Sabine women), would have been another possible fear for a Greco-Roman audience regarding Thecla's safety.[21] Minimally, Thamyris's death assures the audience that his efforts in the first half of the narrative to win her back will not recur. With his death, there is no chance he will reclaim Thecla for marriage or curtail Thecla's freedom of movement as she travels to and from the city at the close of the narrative.

In contrast to the presentation of Thecla's mother and of Alexander, the *ATh* does not indicate that Thamyris tried to harm Thecla or was abusive to her. Nonetheless, Thamyris's refusal to accept Thecla's decision, his controlling behavior, and the language of ownership can be disturbing to readers today in ways different from a Greco-Roman audience. Thamyris's controlling behavior invites reflection on how this aspect of the *ATh* may relate to the danger women face when they choose to reject a man. According to the US Justice Department, women are seventy times more likely to be killed in the period immediately after leaving a partner than at

---

[19] See Lefkowitz and Fant, *Women's Life in Greece and Rome,* sec. 149, 120–21.

[20] For an overview of the betrothal process, bridewealth, dowry, and indirect dowry, see Hanson and Oakman, *Palestine in the Time of Jesus,* 30–34.

[21] Evans-Grubbs, "Abduction Marriage in Antiquity: A Law of Constantine (CTh IX.24.I) and Its Social Context."

any time during the relationship.[22] Given the prevalence of violence against women who break off a relationship with a man, employing a hermeneutic of suspicion, audiences today sometimes wonder what is *not* being said about the man to whom Thecla had been betrothed and had rejected. This question about the dangers women face when breaking off a relationship is rooted in the real experiences of women across time and culture. For an audience today, having Thamyris found dead at the end of the narrative ties up loose ends in ways that go beyond what the text explicitly states and what the author may have intended.

The *ATh* depicts Thecla as a survivor: She survives her mother's efforts to have her immolated to restore family honor; she survives Alexander's repeated attempts to bring about an honor killing; and the story concludes with the audience assured that she will not have to deal with efforts to reclaim gifts, or worse, be a victim of a dowry-related death.[23] Although the text does not indicate anything about the betrothal process, nor does it state that Thamyris sought to recover betrothal gifts, the betrothal gift-giving process and the potential for recouping the exchanges were culturally assumed knowledge in the Greco-Roman world.[24] The recovery of betrothal gifts and marriage abduction are probably not particularly relevant for most people reading this text for the first time today but may well have been on the minds of a Greco-Roman audience.

A final thought concerns how Thamyris's death can be viewed as part of the conversation that the *ATh* is having with 1 Timothy. The deaths of two characters, Falconilla and Thamyris, can be read

---

[22] In addition to the Justice Department, Violence Policy Center (https://vpc.org), see the National Domestic Violence Hotline website (https://www.thehotline.org/identify-abuse/power-and-control).

[23] "Dowry death" is a term that refers to killing a wife to collect another dowry in some countries today. See Roy, *Encyclopedia of Violence Against Women and Dowry Death in India*. We use the term "dowry-related death" rather than simply "dowry death" to acknowledge that the Greco-Roman betrothal-marriage customs are distinct from countries where dowry death occurs today. The cultural differences coalesce, however, in the danger women face.

[24] On early Christian texts as high context documents that presume extensive knowledge of the context on the part of the listening audience, see Rohrbaugh, *The New Testament in Cross-Cultural Perspective*, 8–10.

as an implied rhetorical critique of 1 Timothy: Falconilla dies and is transferred to the abode of the righteous apart from having had children, and had Thecla married Thamyris, his death would have left her unembedded in a man's home, which is to say that the safety the *paterfamilias* affords is precarious in contrast to the safety God ultimately provides. Recall that the *A Th* critiques the subordination to the *paterfamilias* and the notion of female salvation through childbirth found in 1 Timothy (see chapter 4). Thecla is embedded in the household of God, with God as *paterfamilias* and patron.

Further reading about the Greco-Roman context: Lefkowitz and Fant, *Women's Life in Greece and Rome: A Source Book in Translation*; Lemos, *Marriage Gifts and Social Change in Ancient Palestine*; Hanson and Oakman, *Palestine in the Time of Jesus*; Morales, *Antigone Rising*.

On current global contexts: Penn and Nardos, *Overcoming Violence against Women and Girls: The International Campaign to Eradicate a Worldwide Problem*; Roy, *Encyclopedia of Violence Against Women and Dowry Death in India*.

Websites and organizations: National Coalition Against Domestic Violence (https://ncadv.org); World Health Organization (https://www.who.int/health-topics/violence-against-women); National Sexual Violence Resource Center (https://www.nsvrc.org); National Domestic Violence Hotline (https://www.thehotline.org); Rape, Abuse & Incest National Network (http://rainn.org).

For a succinct overview of femicide globally, see the report *Femicide and International Women's Rights* at https://theglobalamericans.org/reports/femicide-international-womens-rights.

Scholars often observe that Paul is feminized and Thecla gradually masculinized. How do you make sense of that discussion?

When the *A Th* begins, Thecla is in a house and Paul is entering the city in the public sphere. By the end of the story, Thecla visits Paul in a house while she is the one traveling and entering a strange city. In this way, the narrative indicates a reversal of gendered locations. Paul begins the narrative teaching in Onesiphoros's house and testifying before the governor in Iconium, but by the end it is Thecla who teaches and testifies publicly before the governor in Antioch. In Greco-Roman culture, a woman's honor was typically attached entirely to her household and role as a member of a family, while male honor increased and decreased in the public eye through various public and social interactions. Thecla's honor increases throughout the narrative and is attached to actions in the public arena, the space particularly associated with male honor. In contrast, Paul disappears from the story during the Antioch chapter, not only leaving Thecla to defend herself but also not responding to Alexander's advances, relinquishing an opportunity to establish his own honor. As already mentioned above, the image of a weaving spider can be read as portraying Paul engaged in a typically female pursuit. The weaving imagery and his passivity when Alexander attacks Thecla is part of the complexity of the depiction of Paul, who also exhibits what Greco-Roman culture considered to be strong masculine characteristics in his public speaking and endurance.

A second example of fluid gender characterization concerns Thecla's efforts to be baptized: She offers to cut her hair (25), and near the end of the narrative she dresses in a male style (40) to travel, at which point she informs Paul that she has been baptized. Thecla does not actually cut her hair in the Greek witnesses, as Rosie Andrious notes, although "other parallel traditions did have Thecla cut her hair and physically masculinize herself in this way."[25] In Andrious's reading, Paul encourages Thecla to "stay female" by discouraging her from cutting her hair, but he also does not accept her into his care, as he denies knowing her to Alexander immediately following this exchange. In fact, Thecla appears female throughout most of the story; her brief appearance in male disguise does not actually relate to her increase in power and honor as the story unfolds. Her male dress is a disguise to protect her honor, as is

---

[25] Andrious, *Saint Thecla*, 72–73. Andrious also notes that the Thecla cult stressed her female gender (74–75), which suggests the Greek tradition of her uncut hair predominated. Cf. Egyptian iconography of Thecla (75, figure 4.1).

the case in the Greek romance *ET* 5.1, where a woman dresses as a man to avoid danger.

Thecla's effort to disguise herself at the end of the story complicates the gender roles in the narrative and relates to the disguise motif in the Greek romances. Rosie Andrious directly addresses this matter in her chapter on "Becoming Male," in which she argues that Thecla undergoes a partial gender transformation but "remains a complex representation of wo/man."[26] She further states, "Apart from her masculinized dress, Thecla is female in body and . . . she displays traditional womanly behavior, but this is at times infused with masculine courage."[27] In agreement with this observation, in both of her persecutions Thecla is naked, highlighting her perceived female sex and gender, and governors weep (22: associated with power; 34: because of her beauty). Yet, as the second trial ends, Thecla displays endurance and bold public speaking, which were considered emblematic of male performance. We caution readers, however, that gender conceptions of the Greco-Roman world are not normative in and of themselves, but are, as Caroline Vander Stichele and Todd Penner note, "*perceived* universal, natural categories of identity in the ancient world."[28] Vander Stichele and Penner assist in thinking about the way the *ATh* depicts Thecla's private and public performances related to social constructions of sex and gender identity.[29]

Moreover, it is not clear how an ancient audience would have reacted to the way the *ATh* depicts Thecla's gender for several reasons, including that Greco-Roman literature is replete with examples of gender performance transgressions. A negative gender transgression concerns Clytemnestra in Aeschylus's *Agamemnon,* who is introduced (11) as "woman in passionate heart and man in strength of purpose," and she is routinely described and behaves in ways associated with men in ancient Athens,[30] whereas the great war

---

[26] Andrious, *Saint Thecla,* 78.

[27] Andrious, *Saint Thecla,* 80.

[28] Vander Stichele and Penner, *Contextualizing Gender,* 63.

[29] Vander Stichele and Penner, *Contextualizing Gender,* 22–23, 216–17.

[30] See the discussion of speech in the Oresteia in McClure, *Spoken Like a Woman,* ch. 3.

hero Agamemnon is depicted as vulnerable, passive, and penetrated—stereotypical female attributes of that culture. While the heroic warrior is typically a male role in the Greco-Roman world, celebrated in *aristeia* scenes of exceptional valor in Homer's *Iliad* and Virgil's *Aeneid*, a notable exception is the virgin warrior Camilla in book 11 of the *Aeneid*, who is introduced by the virgin goddess Diana. Camilla's example is particularly important for reading the *ATh* in an ancient context because women taking on male performance roles was accepted as both anomalous and celebrated, particularly, as is the case with Camilla and Thecla, when the woman is separated from traditional gender roles through embracing virginity with divine approval.

There may have been a theological understanding behind the dynamic of Thecla's increasingly male performance, specifically in relation to the initiation ritual of baptism. As discussed in the box below, some in the Greco-Roman world may have interpreted baptism in light of a reading of Galatians 3:28 that understands baptism as a way for women to become more male when "putting on Christ." In a one-sex model of human beings, femaleness and maleness do not indicate a binary difference, but rather male and female are on a spectrum in which females are biologically inferior males. Read through the lens of a one-sex model of human beings, the *ATh* may depict Thecla as becoming more male as she progresses through her initiation toward baptism.

Box 6: Galatians 3:28, Gender Differentiation, and Thecla Taking on Maleness

Galatians 3:27–28 reads: "For all of you who were baptized into Christ have clothed yourselves with Christ. There is neither Jew nor Greek, there is neither slave nor free person, there is not male and female; for you are all one in Christ Jesus."

As we have seen in chapter 3 regarding Pervo's understanding of the Alexander scene (26), scholars sometimes understand Galatians 3:28 as an essential background text for the plot of the *A Th*. Glenn Snyder also sees the *A Th* as a narrative representation of Galatians 3:27–28.[31] Galatians 3:28 is an important text associated with baptism, and the entire plot of the *A Th* revolves around Thecla seeking to be baptized after she has become enamored with Paul's message about the gospel of self-control and resurrection.

Some scholars read Galatians 3:28 in light of the myth of "primal androgyny," which refers to the idea that God originally created human beings in the garden without distinction between male and female (Gen 1:27 "humankind"); thus, a non-gendered or one-sex state was God's original vision of humanity, a vision being realized again in the baptism ritual referred to in Galatians 3:28: "there is not male and female." A key component of the myth, however, concerns a body-soul dualism in which bodies are divided into sexes, and for some (e.g., Philo, Tertullian) souls also were gendered.[32] Since Paul's genuine letters and the *A Th* lack clear reference to an immortal soul (Phil 1:21–24 being a possible exception), Paul and the author of the *A Th* did not entirely embrace that myth. While Paul at times is negative about the mortal body (Rom 7:24), the *A Th* never develops that aspect of his thinking. In a one-sex model, the phrase "there is not male and female" may presuppose that a baptized female becomes in some sense male as part of the union with Christ, behind which is the idea that maleness reflects a higher spiritual plane than being female (cf. 1 Cor 11:3, 7b). For brief overviews of the debate about ancient constructions of sex and gender and the models that scholars employ to approximate how elite men in the Greco-Roman world conceptualized these matters, see Kraemer, *Unreliable Witnesses*, 14–20; Vander Stichele and Penner, *Contextualizing Gender*, 58–62.

---

[31] Snyder, *Acts of Paul*, 143.
[32] Boyarin, *A Radical Jew*, 185–96.

Since a key expectation of a woman in the Greco-Roman world was that she become a wife and bear children, a perspective thoroughly embraced by the Pastor in 1 Timothy 2:8–15; 5:14, Thecla's transformation through Paul's message of self-control and her refusal to marry are part of a movement away from the traditional female roles in the home and are sometimes seen as a step toward a nongendered or an increasingly masculine state, possibly reflected in Galatians 3:28. Noteworthily, Galatians 3:28 draws on the creation story of Genesis 1, while 1 Timothy 2:8–15 references the creation story of Genesis 2–3 when arguing that women were created second, "for Adam was formed first."

Further reading in addition to those noted above: Boyarin, *A Radical Jew: Paul and the Politics of Identity*, ch. 8; Bassler, *Navigating Paul: An Introduction to Key Theological Concepts*, 45, esp. n62; Snyder, *Acts of Paul*, 139–41.

Regardless of how a Greco-Roman audience might have understood the gender roles in the *ATh*, we can grapple with and appropriate the story in new ways using our own cultural presuppositions and experiences regarding sex and gender. To do so responsibly, we should maintain a critical engagement with the relative nature of our own cultural conceptions of sex and gender.[33] We encourage you to read the story with attention to identity performance and to do further thinking about sex and gender constructions more generally. In addition to the overview of models for understanding sex and gender in the Greco-Roman world noted in the box above, Vander Stichele and Penner have helpful discussions on discourse and social production of knowledge in *Contextualizing Gender in Early Christian Discourse*, 17–40, and in relation to their reading of the *ATh*, see 214–20. See also Kraemer, *Unreliable Witnesses*, 136–43; Andrious, *Saint Thecla*, esp. 66–87.

---

[33] Vander Stichele and Penner, *Contextualizing Gender*, 51.

What motivates Thecla's mother's deep anger at her daughter's refusal to marry Thamyris?

For the modern reader, it is disturbing that Theocleia calls for her daughter to be burned during the trial in Iconium: "Burn the lawless one! Burn the one who refuses to be a bride" (20). From the perspective of her mother, Theocleia, Thecla has deeply damaged the family honor by her refusal to go through with the betrothal, which will result in her not bearing children and not taking an honorable place in the culture as matron of Thamyris's home. Sympathy for Theocleia's anger would likely have been a typical response to the story in the Greco-Roman world; an ancient audience would have seen Thecla as an example of what happens when a girl is not under the control of a father and lacks "the taming effect of marriage."[34]

Moreover, betrothal was an agreement between two families that often extended over a considerable period of time, although the *ATh* never tells us how long Thamyris and Thecla had been paired (sometimes today called an arranged marriage). The arrangement between families may have been confirmed many years prior, perhaps when Thecla's father was still alive, and typically would not take into consideration the children's wishes (e.g., in *Call* 1.1, Callirhoe's father, Hermocrates, agrees to the marriage between her and Chaereas but does not ask his daughter about the matter). The narrative of the *ATh* never tells us anything about the gifts that had been promised or already exchanged as part of the premarriage rituals of dowry and bridewealth, such as, for instance, jewelry.[35] Bruce Malina and Richard Rohrbaugh explain that in the gift giving, a central concern is to balance the honor of each family "and at the same time provide for the needs of the new couple linking the two families."[36] (The only explicit mention of gift giving occurs when Alexander attempts to negotiate with Paul for Thecla because he assumes she is embedded in some way in his house [26].) It is unclear if the gift giving between the couple's family had already been

---

[34] McLarty, *Thecla's Devotion*, 218.
[35] See Misset-van de Weg, "Answers to the Plights," 150.
[36] Malina and Rohrbaugh, *Social-Science Commentary*, 333.

accomplished to some extent or was still mostly promised. If the dowry had already been given, the woman would have to relinquish it to the man (cf. *LC* 8.8). Between elite families, property and other promised gifts could amount to an extensive exchange of wealth.[37]

The arrangements between the families were not only about exchange of wealth and gifts but also concerned the family's honor or public reputation. Unstated but implicit in Theocleia's motives likely include the following: The mother could not fathom why Thecla would renounce the freedom and authority that a married elite matron would yield,[38] nor could she fathom how Thecla could willingly choose to associate with an outsider who has no honor or social standing and in so doing was demonstrating disregard for the destruction of the family honor.[39] Her behavior, shameful to that culture, includes sneaking out at night alone looking for Paul (18–19). Women in that context were expected to have intense concern for family honor that would be exhibited through modest behavior. Theocleia describes Paul to Thamyris as a stranger who "teaches with beguiling and crafty words, so that I am astonished at how this young woman's sense of modesty is so grievously troubled" (8). This understanding of Paul leads to the governor's charge that he is a corruptor of women and a magician (15). Twice the narrator repeats that the mob agreed with that assessment (15, 20). Moreover, Theocleia expected Thecla to produce children who would become heir to Thamyris's considerable wealth (property, animals, slaves) and continue to the upbuilding of the family's honorable reputation. When Thecla returns to Iconium at the end of the story, it is for good reason that she tells her mother (43), "If you long for wealth, God[40]

---

[37] On betrothal, see also Campbell, ed., *Marriage and Family in the Biblical World*, esp. 185–87.

[38] Hylen, *A Modest Apostle*, 85.

[39] In *LC* 6.13, Sosthenes considers Leucippe's rejection of wealth, marriage, luxury, and a husband — all of which comes if she marries Thersandros — to be an indication that she is an incurable raging maniac.

[40] There is no definite article ("the") in the Greek text of Lipsius, which reads "a Lord." In that case, "Lord" can refer to any patron, divine or human. However, the forthcoming critical Greek edition (Appendix 1) reads, "God will give them [riches] to you." It would seem that the change to "Lord" was intended to include human patronage.

will give it to you through me. If (you long for) a child, look, here I am!" The story ends with Thecla's rebuttal of two aspects of her mother's concerns about the losses occasioned by her daughter's strange behavior and unexpected choices.

Finally, Theocleia claims that Paul's message is a threat to the city (9), which Thamyris repeats with the additional assertion that Paul corrupts the city (*polis*) and young women such as Thecla. These claims reflect the view that the home (*oikos*) is a metaphor for the larger public sphere, a microcosm of the *polis*,[41] and thus the destruction of family life is by extension destruction of the *polis*. Theocleia, therefore, saw Thecla's actions as larger than simply her daughter disobeying her wishes. Crucially, the crowd of married women provide a rebuttal of the claim that Thecla's actions harm the *polis* in the Antioch segment (28, 32).

What do you make of Paul's words to Thecla in section 41 regarding Thecla's ministry?

When Paul finally speaks in support of Thecla's ministry in 41, he says simply, "Go and teach the word of God." It is worth examining more closely what Paul does and does not say to Thecla in this crucial scene.

Paul's words are somewhat ambiguous because he does not specifically tell her to teach anyone, men or women. Given that the Pastor forbade women to teach men, this ambiguity is important. The Pastor did not forbid women to teach other women, and Paul in section 41 does not clarify what is meant by his endorsement of her teaching. Notably, in section 39, when Thecla teaches Tryphaena and her household, the text specifies female slaves: "Thecla went with her and rested in her home for eight days, teaching her the word of God with the result that most of the female slaves also came to believe, and there was a great joy in the home." Paul in the *A Th* does not actually endorse a public apostolic ministry absent male accompaniment. If one looks carefully at his genuine letters, Paul mentions women who are in leadership roles, such as the deacon

---

[41] Ault, "Living in the Classical *Polis.*" Cf. Aristotle, *Politics* 1.1253b1–12, 1260b9–20.

and patron Phoebe, but the text says nothing about them having an itinerant apostolic ministries.

Thecla herself does not initially seek a ministry apart from Paul; she asks to be with him in his ministry (25), and her words there highlight the element of gender in public apostolic ministry: "I will cut my hair and follow you wherever you may go." The heart of the matter is that women clearly did not often engage in itinerant apostolic ministry, and when they did, they did not do so unaccompanied by men. That point may seem obvious given what we know of the dangers of travel in the Greco-Roman world and the fact that itinerant apostles like Paul experienced imprisonment.[42] Particularly illuminating in this regard is Junia, who is "prominent among the apostles" (Rom 16:7). Paul refers to her and Andronicus as "my fellow prisoners." Clearly, Andronicus and Junia were neither executed nor enslaved as a result of their imprisonment, as Paul would then not direct greetings to them.

Box 7: Prisons in the Greco-Roman World

There is not much evidence concerning prisons in the Greco-Roman world of the first two centuries. In Rome in the late Republic during the Catiline Conspiracy (63 BCE), the elite conspirators were not held in the same places as the non-elite but rather with senators. With some exceptions, elites were punished by exile or confiscation of property or were encouraged to commit suicide. Punishment for non-elites included enslavement, re-enslavement in the case of freed persons, or execution. Prisons generally were designated to hold non-elites awaiting trial or the condemned temporarily before execution. Indications of elite status in relation to prisons in the *ATh* include the following: Thecla is allowed to stay in Tryphaena's home rather than prison, Paul is allowed visitors in prison, Thecla bribes the guard with expensive items to visit Paul, and Paul is expelled from the

---

[42] On the anxiety that female travel produced, see Kraemer, *Unreliable Witnesses*, 254–55.

city. In *Leucippe and Clitophon*, the elite Thersandros is exiled (8.15), whereas the slave Sosthenes is imprisoned. In the *AP* 9.20, prison is described as cramped and gloomy.

Further reading: Peters, "Prison before the Prison: The Ancient and Medieval Worlds," esp. 13–21; Robinson, *Penal Practice and Penal Policy in Ancient Rome*, 113–15; Millar, "Condemnation to Hard Labour in the Roman Empire, from the Julio-Claudians to Constantine."

Paul does not want to take Thecla with him on his itinerant ministry journeys. He gives the following reason (25): "The present age is shameful and you are beautiful. [I fear that] another trial will overtake you, worse than the first, and you may not endure [it] but behave cowardly." It is likely that the original audience would have understood that Paul is trying to protect her from the sorts of things that happen to him or those who are awaiting sentencing in the Roman system. See chapter 3 on patronage for further discussion of that text.

Although Thecla initially seeks to engage in an itinerant apostolic ministry with Paul (25), and twice goes out looking for him, as the story draws to a close, she informs Paul of what she is going to do (41: "I am going to Iconium"). Then Paul affirms her role as a teacher, but the text does not clarify whom he endorses her to teach. That ambiguity may be deliberate given the attitude some Christians had about women teaching men, as can be seen from the Pastor's remarks (1 Tim 2:12). The story ends, however, with a subtle disambiguation with the word "many": Thecla "enlightened many with the word of God." The Greek word is masculine plural, so the original audience would naturally conclude that her teaching ministry included men.[43]

---

[43] Recall from chapter 1 that Tertullian's admonition of the Thecla text indicates that some were interpreting Thecla's ministry as license for women to baptize and as an example for their own ministry. Paul's approval of Thecla's apostolic teaching ministry in *ATh* 41 was also mentioned implicitly in Tertullian's admonition as problematic.

Questions and Responses: Theology and Spirituality

What does the ATh *say and not say about resurrection and afterlife?*

Resurrection is one of the two pillars of Paul's opening speech, even though resurrection is not explicitly mentioned in the beatitudes (see the beatitudes question above).

The *ATh* contains several references to the afterlife, none more interesting than Thecla's prayer for Falconilla's transition to the place of the righteous (28–29). Thecla's prayer refers to the hope that Falconilla will "live forever" (twice in 29), and in her response to the governor, Thecla states that those who do not believe in the Son "will not live but will die forever" (37). There are several references to heaven in the *ATh* (21, 22, 24, 29, and 43), but none of them are used to describe where Falconilla is after her death or what "a place of the righteous" might mean. In her prayer for Falconilla, Thecla addresses "My God, the Son of the Most High who is in heaven" (29) and asks for eternal life for Falconilla — but what exactly that means is also not explained. Moreover, Falconilla was not baptized, and so her transference to the place of the righteous is in some tension with the statement in 37: "Whoever does not believe in Him will not live but will die forever." This tension is never resolved in the narrative but coheres with the Pastor's statement in 1 Timothy 4:10 that the living God is "savior of all, especially of those who believe." As noted in chapter 4, the author of the *ATh* and the Pastor seem to agree that it is possible for those who do not believe to have the living God as their savior.

As is often the case in the *ATh*, we do not get very much information that would help us with our further questions. In this instance, the story tells us nothing about how Falconilla died. Culturally, transition to the abode of the dead (Hades and Tartaros for Greeks)[44] was related to proper burial. The unburied were at risk

---

[44] Virgil's *Aeneid* 6.322–29 reflects the Greco-Roman view that the unburied cannot cross to the abode of the dead, inherited from the *Iliad* 11.50–54; 23.65–74. Regarding an in-between state in 1 Enoch 22, where the dead are in storage or holding pens, see Segal, *Life After Death*, 277–80. Trumbower examines 1 Peter 3:19–20; 4:5–7, *Apocalypse of Peter* 14:1–4, and *Passion of Perpetua and Felicitas* 7–8 (*Rescue for the Dead*, 44–55, 80–85). Cf. Revelation 6:9–11 (martyrs await God's action).

of being in a vague and undefined in-between place. Although the abode of the dead was not a happy place, at least it was not no place. It is unclear whether Falconilla is in the abode of the dead or in an in-between place; the narrative only says that she wants to go to the place of the righteous. The lack of clarity on these matters is further complicated by Tryphaena saying after Thecla survives the arena, "Now I believe that the dead are raised. Now I believe that my child lives" (39). Here we see a mixing of transference and resurrection without further clarification.

Further reading on this topic: Trumbower, *Rescue for the Dead: The Posthumous Salvation of Non-Christians in Early Christianity*, esp. ch. 3; Segal, *Life After Death: A History of the Afterlife in Western Religion*, 277–80, 359, 591; Rordorf, "La Prière de sainte Thècle pour une dèfunte païenne et son importance oecuménique."

How does the ATh *compare with the rest of the Acts of Paul in which it is embedded? What corollaries and tensions are there between the two originally distinct works?*

Recalling the diagram from the introduction, we remind you that the *ATh* is part of a larger text, the *Acts of Paul*. There are several important connections between the *ATh* and the larger *AP* in which it is embedded. These include

- **Female discipleship.** Thecla as a female disciple of Paul's finds a partial parallel with Eubula, a married freedwoman in *AP* 9.16 whose name means "well-advised, prudent" and who is referred to as "a disciple of Paul and attached herself to him day and night." Thecla is similarly described as "listening night and day to the word about purity spoken by Paul." It is possible that the Eubula story is an addition to the *AP*,[45] perhaps added at the same time as the *ATh*. There are several stories in the *AP* about women, some of them married, who become Paul's disciples, which relates to the reference in *ATh* 7 to "many women and girls" seeking out Paul's message.

---

[45] See Pervo's discussion in *The Acts of Paul*, 234–36.

- **Window location when listening to Paul.** Just as the *ATh* repeatedly emphasizes that Thecla hears Paul from a window (five times in 7–9), Patroclus also listens to Paul "perched in a high window" (*AP* 14.1). Both Thecla and Patroclus are delivered from death and testify before powerful Roman authorities.
- **Epithets.** Just as Thecla is "slave of God" (26, 37), so Paul is "slave of the Lord" (*AP* 12.5 // Col 4:7; 2 Tim 2:24) and "slave of Christ" (*AP* 9.27 // Rom 1:1; Gal 1:10). God is given the epithet "the living God" (*ATh* 17, 37 // *AP* 6.4; 9.17; 13.6; 14.4 [twice], 5). The two epithets combined, "slave of the living God," occur in *ATh* 37.
- **Rival teachings.** In both stories there is a dispute with rival teachings on resurrection, with Demas and Hermogenes (14) maintaining that "resurrection has already happened when we have children" // *AP* 10.1: The message of Simon and Cleobius is "there is no resurrection of the flesh but [only] of the spirit, and the human body is not a divine creation" (cf. *AP* 10.2).
- **Ascetic concern for sexual renunciation.** *ATh* 5: "Blessed are those who keep the flesh undefiled, for they will become temples of God"; *ATh* 6: "Blessed are the bodies of virgins, for they [their bodies] will please God and they will not lose the reward of their purity" // *AP* 9.9: The lion, after Paul had baptized him, would not look at the lioness. The *AP* never states whether married couples embrace chastity. *AP* 9.13 denounces the pursuit of pleasure; *AP* 10.11 states that human flesh is bound to lust.
- **Ascetic concern for fasting.** *ATh* 23 // *AP* 6.5; 9.27; 12.2–5; 13.1. (No mention of wine in relation to eucharist or eucharistic imagery in *ATh* 25 // *AP* 12.5.)
- **Endurance of suffering.** Just as Thecla's endurance is highlighted in the *ATh*, so also is Paul's (*AP* 12.1–2; 13.7).
- **Baptism related to being "sealed."** *ATh* 25 // *AP* 14.5, 7.
- **Emphasis on the distribution of wealth.** *ATh* 41 // *AP* 5.5 (negative view of wealth in *AP* 9.13, 17; 14.3).

Some points of contrasts between the *A Th* and the *AP* include the following:

- **Miracles.** Paul is a miracle worker in the *AP*, whereas human beings in the *A Th* do not perform miracles. Miraculous intervention in the *A Th* is exclusively tied to God and Jesus's actions. Moreover, Thecla's transformation (to avoid problematic associations with the term "conversion") occurs through Paul's teachings rather than through miraculous deeds, as commonly is the case in the Apocryphal Acts.[46] However, just as the Lord's miracles foster belief in the *AP* 13.11, so Tryphaena comes to believe after God delivers Thecla from death (39). In the fifth-century *Life of Thecla*, she is a miracle worker.

- **Grace.** The *A Th* refers to grace twice, in the description of Paul (3) and in a greeting (4: "grace be with you"), in contrast to the several references to grace in the *AP* (6.1; 9.6, 9, 11, 23, 27; 12.2, 5; 13.1, 4). The Syriac form adds a reference to grace in the opening paragraph of the *A Th*: "But Paul was looking for the dwelling place of the Messiah's grace and was not doing them [Demas and Hermogenes] any harm."

- **Soul.** The *A Th* has no reference to an immortal soul, whereas in the *AP* we find an allusion to Matthew 10:28 at *AP* 9.13: "Your authority extends only to my body . . . but you have no power to kill my soul." Whereas the *A Th* embraces a transcendence of the world without any notion of a platonic soul,[47] that line of the *AP* invites the audience to read the message of transcendence of the world in a way congenial to a body-soul dualism. The *AP* nonetheless adheres to a bodily resurrection (*AP* 10.27, 32).

---

[46] Bremmer, "Conversion in the Oldest Apocryphal Acts," esp. 190–96. Thecla, however, has "power" within her (*A Th* 22).

[47] A Syriac form of the *A Th* adds a reference to soul at the beatitudes in 6: "Blessed are the bodies and souls of virgins, for they will please God." The Syriac also rephrases another beatitude in 6 from "Blessed are those who depart from the appearance of the world for the sake of the love of God" to "Blessed are they who for the love of God have gone out of this body."

- **The holy Spirit.** The *ATh* never mentions the holy Spirit,[48] whereas the holy Spirit plays an important role in Paul's genuine letters and is present in the Pastoral Epistles (1 Tim 4:1; 2 Tim 1:14; Titus 3:5) and the *AP*.[49] In Paul's letters, the holy Spirit is Paul's solution to the problem of desire: Self-control is a fruit of the holy Spirit (Gal 5:23). It is intriguing that the *ATh* emphasizes self-control but nowhere mentions Paul's solution to the problem of desire. The reason for the omission is unclear. One possibility is that the author of the *ATh* wanted to avoid appearing in any way associated with Montanism, a late second-century movement that combined an intense asceticism with spirit-inspired female prophetic leaders.[50] Like Thecla, the female leaders of that movement, Priscilla and Maximilla, rejected marriage and household management and were known for experiencing visions. Although Paul's genuine letters, the Acts of the Apostles, and the *AP* demonstrate divine power acting in the world through the Spirit, the author of the *ATh* was able to display divine power without reference to the Spirit.

In sum, whoever added the *ATh* to the *AP* was able to create several connections to the larger narrative, including an emphasis on female discipleship, asceticism, and endurance and an incorporation of shared epithets and motifs (e.g., window location). Although it is interesting that the *ATh* never refers to the holy Spirit, the reason for the omission remains elusive. To some extent, the Syriac form of the story addresses the omission, which indicates a recognition of the

---

[48] A Syriac form of the *ATh* adds a reference to the Spirit of God at 3.22 as the reason the flames of the fire never harmed her ("because the Spirit of God had compassion on her").

[49] *AP* 10.5: "into whom the Father sent the spirit from heaven"; 10.10: "the spirit of Christ"; 10.13: "and sent the Spirit"; 10.32: "and Spirit of Christ"; 12.2: "Filled with the Holy Spirit, Paul said"; 12.3: "Cleobius, speaking through the Spirit"; 12.5: "the Spirit fell upon Myrta" and "the Spirit within Myrta"; 13.6: "the Spirit of the Christ"; 13.7: "a spirit of power into flesh"; 14.1: "Paul learned of this through the Spirit."

[50] Schüssler Fiorenza, "Word, Spirit and Power," 42, notes that the literature against the Montanists focused attacks particularly on the leadership of women. See also Schüssler Fiorenza, *In Memory of Her*, 300–303.

absence in the earlier forms of the *A Th*. We have speculated that perhaps the author wanted to avoid associations between Thecla the visionary and teacher and the charismatic female leaders of Montanism, as the Montanists were active in Asia Minor at the time the *A Th* was likely composed and there was already a shared association with asceticism.

Studies of Montanism include: Thomas, "The Scriptures and the New Prophecy: Montanism as Exegetical Crisis"; Tabbernee, *Montanist Inscriptions and Testimonia: Epigraphic Sources Illustrating the History of Montanism*; Trevett, *Montanism, Gender, Authority and the New Prophecy*; Mitchell, "An Epigraphic Probe into the Origins of Montanism"; cf. Heine, *The Montanist Oracles and Testimonia*.

The ATh *has a lot of miracles, some of which seem highly improbable to many people in the twenty-first century. How do you understand the miraculous in the* ATh*?*

It is important to note that Thecla comes to faith through hearing, not through miraculous deeds. That point indicates that the *A Th* is circumspect about the miraculous as a means of coming to Christian faith in a way similar to the Gospel of Mark, where Jesus's first disciples follow him because he calls them—before he has done anything miraculous.

The cascade of miracles that occur in the public spectacles in the *A Th* is also common to the New Testament, Christian martyr literature outside the New Testament, and the Greek romances, which is to say that the author of the *A Th* inherited the miraculous from the stories that influenced the work. It is also important to note that people in the ancient world tended to view the metaphysical (events outside the bounds of rational explanation) as in some sense revelatory of the will of the gods and of hidden realities all around them. The Greek romances are full of divine interventions that affect the course of events in the plot and reveal divine concern for the leading character.[51] Just as Pan and the nymphs intervene to assist

---

[51] Kee, *Miracle in the Early Christian World*, 254.

Daphnis and Chloe and Isis delivers Habrocomes and Antheia, so Thecla's God delivers her. Further reading: Kee, *Miracle in the Early Christian World*, ch. 8.

A postcolonial lens can be helpful for analyzing the miraculous. Postcolonial interpretation views a text from the vantage point of more than five hundred years of European colonization, genocide, and subordination of indigenous peoples. From the beginning of colonization, European colonial thinking about the miraculous in their own sacred stories was used to denigrate the different epistemologies (ways of understanding what constitutes knowledge) and foreign stories that the colonizers encountered. Indigenous ways of knowing and spiritualities have long prized and still prize stories that reveal spiritual and material dimensions of the world in a variety of creative and profound ways that are not necessarily able to be verified historically or scientifically. Indigenous stories characteristically weave the metaphysical into storytelling and predate the period of colonization by many thousands of years. Since the start of colonization, storytelling has been an important way of continuing indigenous culture and countering efforts to destroy indigenous people and their cultures. Part of the process of colonization has been eradicating indigenous stories and storytellers, a two-pronged genocide: the killing of people and the destruction of a culture. On these matters, see the works of George Tinker, including *American Indian Liberation: A Theology of Sovereignty*, and the National Native American Boarding School Healing Coalition website,[52] which contains links related to education, healing, and advocacy.

The message in the *ATh* that God protects and delivers Thecla counters the claims of Greco-Roman culture that power resides with the Roman empire, its gods, and its representatives, such as Alexander. Although the *ATh* shows a sensitivity to not entirely denigrating the Roman imperial governors — depicting them as receptive to and sympathetic towards Paul and Thecla — the strikingly negative depiction of Alexander as patron of the imperial

---

[52] https://boardingschoolhealing.org/

games speaks to the way the miraculous in the *A Th* is an aspect of countering the Roman ideology of power. This understanding of miracles as a part of a counternarrative does not mean accepting that the text's metaphysical claims reflect historical events; rather, focusing on the miraculous as counternarrative can assist in seeing rhetorical features of a story, ancient or modern.

Is there any indication of progression in Thecla's faith and spiritual life in the A Th?

Yes. The text states explicitly so at 7 ("she advanced in faith with abundant joy") and 18 ("with her faith growing, she kept kissing his chains"). Thecla's emotional response to Paul's teaching is evident with kissing the chains, which relates to *An Ephesian Tale* 2.8, where Antheia visits Habrocomes in prison and "kissed him, embraced him, clung to his chains and rolled at his feet."[53] A significant and revealing change occurs when the narrator links Thecla's emotional response in 18 to her growth in faith. A similar emotional reaction occurs when Thecla takes leave of Paul to return to Iconium at the end of the story (42), where she falls on the ground and weeps while praying at the spot where Paul used to teach in Onesiphoros's house. Both texts, 20 and 42, connect Thecla's emotional response of deep gratitude specifically to Paul's teaching. However, the language in 20, derived from *An Ephesian Tale*, resembles an infatuation even with the link to Paul as teacher, whereas her response in 42 does not stop with her esteem for the person whose teaching brought her to the faith but is coupled with a prayer that directs her gratitude to her patron, God, and God's broker, Christ Jesus, her helper in her trials. Moreover, it is important, as McLarty notes, that Thecla initiates her parting with Paul (41).[54] Thecla is now a Christian in her own right, with her own ministry. Finally, Thecla grows from silence — albeit a silence that was considered a virtue for women — to publicly testifying in the course of the narrative after having endured many

---

[53] The Heidelberg Coptic omits kissing the chains, likely considering that behavior to be embarrassing.

[54] McLarty, *Thecla's Devotion*, 86

trials. A Greco-Roman audience would have considered her silence and endurance to be strong virtues.

Thecla's growth in the stages of faith into discipleship has some analogue with Gloria Anzaldúa's seven stages in the path of *conocimiento* (awareness),[55] which include the following:

1. A jolt from the familiar and safe that causes the person to rethink everything.
2. A transitional in-between space (*nepantla*) allows the person to see new perspectives and have moments of critical awareness; the old way of seeing the world and the new way co-exist.
3. Existing in competing epistemologies results in hopelessness, distress, even paralysis.
4. The person seeks ways of initiating the process to leave behind stage three.
5. The person explores different meanings and attempts to create new forms of thinking.
6. Sharing the new narrative with others tests the narrative.
7. The final stage, spiritual activism, is a space for cooperation, negotiation of conflict and difference, and building alliances.

Thecla undergoes these stages to some degree in the *ATh*. Her jolt occurs when she hears Paul from her window in the safe confines of her home. She enters into a period of silence where she is seemingly trying to understand this new way of viewing the world. When Paul departs, she enters into a form of distress, continually looking for him (21: "like a lamb in the desert looking around for the shepherd"). Thecla tries to initiate the process of baptism despite Paul's demurral (25) and succeeds in baptizing herself (34). She shares the new narrative publicly in the arena (37) in response to the governor's questions. She engages in spiritual activism in her work with Tryphaena, Onesiphoros, and the people of Seleucia. The story ends

---

[55] *Borderlands/La Frontera: The New Mestiza*, 70–113, 237–39; "Now let us shift," 540–78, esp. 544–49.

with her testifying to her mother, negotiating conflict and difference, by offering her mother a different way of viewing the world.

What does the ATh *assert about transcending "the world"?*

Paul's speech to the governor refers to "a wayward world" (17) as part of the theological worldview in which the message about self-control and resurrection assists the audience to transcend the world through present asceticism in the hope of future reward. A message about transcending the world is found in Gentile spirituality of the Greco-Roman world, for instance, in the Hermetic literature (regarding the revelations of the god Hermes), which sharply distinguishes the good and holy divine realm from the flawed earthly realm as well as advances a body-soul dualism.[56] The second-century Hermetic literature, called *Poimandres*, teaches that the body and its desires are negative, while the soul is holy and immortal. Transcendence of the world and the body requires a rebirth through knowledge, which is connected to light and results in embracing an ascetic life. While there are strong disjunctions between the *ATh* and Hermetic teachings, particularly insofar as the *ATh* has no body-soul dualism, Paul's speech in *ATh* 17 has interesting connections with that literature, including the notion that God is "in need of nothing" (*Poimandres* VI.16: "God lacks nothing") and that God's messengers reveal a special knowledge, which in the *ATh* is a knowledge of "dignified behavior and love of truth" that assists adherents in transcending the world and bodily desires (*Poimandres* XIV.1) and move toward light (*ATh* 6: "those who possess the insight of Jesus Christ" will be in light).[57] These connections to Hermetic literature only tell us that Paul's speech to the governor in *ATh* 17 would have made sense to Gentiles who were acquainted with the ascetic impulse and transcendent dualism of Hermetic literature. Not surprisingly, the *ATh* depicts the governor as open to hearing more (17: "until there might be an opportunity for a more thorough hearing").

---

[56] See Johnson, *Among the Gentiles*, 85–92.

[57] In the *Acts of Paul* 9.20, Paul's body illuminates the path — a not very subtle symbolic association of his role as mediator of divine knowledge.

But resonance is not direct influence. Despite these resonances with Hermetic literature, the most direct influence on the theology and ethics of Paul's speech in *A Th* 17 is New Testament texts that encourage an ascetic withdrawal or distancing from "the world" and desires (e.g., 1 John 2:15–17; Gal 6:14) and an embrace of "love of truth" (2 Thess 2:10).

Questions and Responses: Reclaiming the *Acts of Thecla* Today
Is the ATh *a feminist work?*

The question we are asked most frequently is whether this text points to an early feminist movement in the Christian communities. Much to the disappointment of many who first encounter the Thecla story, a response to this question is not straightforward. The narrative is complicated, both in regard to a message of female liberation and with other obstacles to appropriation. Some may find it comforting that there have always been stories and examples of women who demand an equal standing before God. It is certainly frustrating that while there have always been voices demanding consideration, these voices are not always listened to.[58]

One of the techniques of feminist scholarship is to retrieve and celebrate women from Christian history and amplify their voices. We certainly hope that we have done that here. Thecla was a popular figure in some Christian circles for centuries, and we hope to be part of bringing her voice back into people's theological imaginations. How you as a reader decide to appropriate Thecla, either as a strong person who subverted the increasingly male dominated landscape of Christianity or as an obedient figurehead who represented self-discipline and adherence to a particular form of encratic teachings (message of self-control), is up to you. There is a both/and available as well. We can accept the complex nature of storytelling and retrieve our own meanings outside of the constraints of the narrative's setting while also appreciating the scholarship on ancient cultures and influences. There are a variety of interpretative options.

---

[58] On the idea of voices marginalized or not listened to ("listenedless"), see Elenes, "Nepantla, Spiritual Activism, New Tribalism: Chicana Feminist Transformative Pedagogies and Social Justice Education," 136.

That said, the *A Th* was not a second-century social commentary on women's "rights." The text was not arguing for the social equality of women generally, nor would the audience or author have had any sense of what "equal rights" would mean. This text does not uncover a proto-feminist movement either inside the early communities or in the social structures of its time and place. There are several complicating factors to appropriating the text as liberative. As Ross Shepard Kraemer notes, there is a lack of historical first-person sources on women's experience, and the *A Th* is part of that larger problem. Not only is the *A Th* very likely an example of "men writing women," but the narrative also often depicts Thecla as operating in ways congenial to the normative patriarchal culture in which it is embedded, such as the depiction of her as modestly silent (despite the multiple ways of viewing her silence), the legitimation of her ministry by a male (Paul), and reference to God as Father. In the following question we will further examine the problems in the text with violence, social status, and slavery.

For further reading on feminist appropriation, see: Vander Stichele and Penner, *Contextualizing Gender in Early Christian Discourse*; Zamfir, "The Topos of Female Hiddenness," 475–87; Holmes, *Gender: Antiquity and its Legacy*; Kraemer, *Unreliable Witnesses*; Osiek and MacDonald, *A Woman's Place*; Schüssler Fiorenza, *In Memory of Her*; Schneiders, *Women and the Word*; Ahmed, *Living a Feminist Life*; Butler, *Gender Trouble: Feminism and the Subversion of Identity*.

What are other obstacles for appropriation today?

Feminist criticism today scrutinizes texts to highlight the intersection of race, class, and gender, engaging with a multiplicity of concerns in what is commonly referred to as a gender-critical approach. Primary obstacles to a liberative feminist lens or a gender-critical appropriation today include but are not limited to the incredible violence in the narrative, the complicating factor that the elite status of the characters bring, and the presentation of slavery as unquestioned and normative.

Violence against women is exemplified when Thecla's legs are tied to two bulls in order for her to be torn apart. Rosie Andrious refers to that scene as particularly gratuitous:

> Such an image is humiliating even for any modern-day woman, and it would have been especially so for a woman steeped in an antique culture of honour and shame. Surely, such representation bears all the hallmarks of patriarchy, of men writing women, and could not be further from affirming female subjectivity. Reading with a hermeneutic of suspicion shows explicitly and unreservedly that there is a need for caution before claiming such a text is female affirming.[59]

An uncritical reading of the violence against Thecla and the normalization of violence as a standard plot point are problematic. For us today, the violent spectacles in the *ATh* can be an opportunity to think about a variety of related matters, including violence against women, the prison industrial complex (PIC), the policies and laws that created and sustain the PIC, the disproportionate brutalization and incarceration of BIPOC (Black, Indigenous, and People of Color), and cell phone video spectacles. While the cell phone is an important tool to draw attention to police brutality, as is clear from Darnella Frazier's award winning video of George Floyd's murder, there can be a spectacle-like quality to these videos. To counter that problem, we recommend analysis of the videos vis-à-vis the systemic racism that produces the brutalization, dehumanization, and normalization of violence. We write this introductory book in Minneapolis and St. Louis Park respectively, not far from George Floyd Square, Say Their Names Cemetery, and the Fort Snelling concentration camp at Bdote.[60]

Further reading: Richardson, *Bearing Witness While Black: African Americans, Smartphones, and the New Protest #Journalism*;

---

[59] See Andrious, *Saint Thecla*, 124, see also ch. 5.

[60] See Johnson, "A Salute to Three Heroines of George Floyd Square." Regarding Say Their Names Cemetery, see George Floyd Street Art at the Urban Anti-racist Street Art Mapping website, https://georgefloydstreetart.omeka.net/items/show/1607. Regarding Fort Snelling, see Waziyatawin, *What Does Justice Look Like?*

Baker, *Humane Insight: Looking at Images of African American Suffering and Death*; Fidel, "The Dangerous Spectacle of Racist Violence Viral Videos"; Cone, *The Cross and the Lynching Tree*; Douglas, *Stand Your Ground: Black Bodies and the Justice of God*; Davis, ed., *Policing the Black Man: Arrest, Prosecution and Imprisonment*; Ralph, *The Torture Letters: Reckoning with Police Violence*; see the Critical Resistance website (https://criticalresistance.org) and the Black Lives Matter website (https://blacklivesmatter.com).

The elite status of Thecla and Tryphaena complicate analysis of the text insofar as their social status afforded them freedoms that would not have been available to most women in the Greco-Roman world. They are not actually representative of the concerns of average women. Just as today, economic security can prevent someone from seeing social evil, such is the case with the characters in the *ATh*, who take slavery for granted as unquestioned and normative. Thecla is able to break out of her elite bubble only to some extent. Born into an elite family, the plot revolves around her mother's desire that she continue her privileged status through her arranged marriage. Indeed, Thecla appeals to her status when Alexander attacks her. Otherwise, Thecla gives up everything in order to follow Paul. It is noteworthy, however, that the story ends with her return to privilege through inheritance of Tryphaena's wealth, which follows a trope of the Greek romances. Although Tryphaena uses her position as an elite to protect Thecla and end the games, she effectively never surrenders her incredibly high status.

A way to look at Thecla's elite status for critical appropriation today is perhaps to think about how women of privilege can be inspired by Thecla's bravery and willingness to step out of the comfort and safety of home. Such bravery is similar to Viola Gregg Liuzzo, who left her family to join the civil rights movement and was murdered by Klansmen on March 25, 1965. She is among the many Civil Rights martyrs whose stories can be viewed online at the Civil Rights Memorial.[61]

---

[61] https://www.splcenter.org/what-we-do/civil-rights-memorial/civil-rights-martyrs

Viola Gregg Liuzzo could have remained in the stability of married life, but she left her family because she had a sense of the urgency regarding the evil of systemic racism in the US. Just as most privileged European Americans were unwilling to risk anything in the fight for social justice and the unmasking of systemic racism, so most elite women in the Greco-Roman world would not have chosen Thecla's path and would have considered it extremely reckless. Today we have courageous women continuing to struggle for social justice, including the founders of Black Lives Matter, Alicia Garza, Patrisse Cullors, and Opal Tometi.

We have already alluded to the problem of the normative representation of slavery. The enslaved people in Thecla's household in Iconium are represented as amplifying her mother's concern and worry (10); they are part of Tryphaena's household, with one of the female slaves perhaps playing the trickster role when she shouts that Tryphaena had died of shock at the arena to save Thecla (36); and they travel with Thecla to find Paul (40). It is difficult to argue that the text subverts social systems while it depicts slavery as normative. Since slavery is unethical, it presents challenges to reading the text as liberative in other ways. This same problem recurs, of course, in the New Testament. These ancient texts provide an opportunity to reflect on the sins of inequality, inequity, and the roots of our systemic injustices today. See Smith and Kim, "Roman Slavery and the New Testament," 45–50; Glancy, *Slavery as a Moral Problem*.

Clearly, there are problematic aspects of the *ATh* that ought not be ignored. If we engage them honestly, we will be better able to confront related or similar problems in our own time. The *ATh* can be deeply inspirational for women who are looking for their own voice in faith communities that do not allow or curtail female leadership. Examined in tandem with 1 Timothy 2:8–15, the *ATh* assists us in asking important theological questions about salvation. The *ATh* can help us in framing questions important for us today regarding the full inclusion of women, LGBTQ+ people, and any group denied equal access to leadership and inclusion that a liberative theology envisions. We argued in chapter 4 that the theological message around salvation concerns egalitarian access to the principles and teachings of the Christ movement. In contrast to the Pastor's perspective (1 Tim 2:15), salvation does not change based on one's gender in the *ATh*.

For further reading: Womanist theology assists thinking about salvation more expansively. See, for instance, Coleman, *Making a Way out of No Way*, ch. 1. Regarding individualism as an inherent problem of salvation, see Tinker, *American Indian Liberation*, esp. 77–78, 99–103.

In addition to obstacles, exploring difficult aspects of ancient texts is also an opportunity to develop an adult faith that acknowledges and contextualizes shifts, some detrimental, in the history of Christianity. In that regard, it is important to understand that the *ATh* was composed at a time in which Christianity was a minority and sometimes persecuted faith. It would be several centuries before the momentous change that happened under Constantine, Roman emperor from 307–337, who made Christianity the religion of the state, an event that marked a major shift in power and privilege for Christianity. Thecla's testimony to her mother at the end of the narrative, in which she asks her mother to consider a Christian epistemology, may look different when viewed from the perspective of a persecuted minority pre-Constantine than after the Crusades of conquest, the Middle Passages, and centuries of Christian genocidal colonization against indigenous peoples.

For further reading, see Robinson, *Race and Theology*; Jennings, *The Christian Imagination* and *After Whiteness*; Wilson-Hartgrove, *Reconstructing the Gospel*; Du Mez, *Jesus and John Wayne*; Massingale, *Racial Justice and the Catholic Church*.

What are some excellent, accessible secondary resources for further study of the ATh?

Hylen, Susan E. *A Modest Apostle: Thecla and the History of Women in the Early Church*. Oxford: Oxford University Press, 2015.

Klauck, Hans-Josef. *The Apocryphal Acts of the Apostles: An Introduction.* Waco: Baylor University Press, 2008.

Kraemer, Ross Shepard. "Thecla." In *The Oxford Handbook of New Testament, Gender, and Sexuality*, edited by Benjamin H. Dunning, 485–503. Oxford: Oxford University Press, 2019.

———. *Unreliable Witnesses: Religion, Gender, and History in the Greco-Roman Mediterranean.* Oxford: Oxford University Press, 2011.

MacDonald, Margaret Y. *Early Christian Women and Pagan Opinion: The Power of the Hysterical Woman.* Cambridge, UK: Cambridge University Press, 1996.

McGinn, Sheila. "The Acts of Thecla." In *Searching the Scriptures: A Feminist Commentary*, edited by Elisabeth Schüssler Fiorenza with the assistance of Ann Brock and Shelly Matthews, 800–828. New York: Crossroad, 1994.

McLarty, J. D. *Thecla's Devotion: Narrative, Emotion and Identity in the Acts of Paul and Thecla.* Cambridge, UK: James Clarke & Co, 2018.

Osiek, Carolyn, and Margaret Y. MacDonald with Janet H. Tulloch. *A Woman's Place: House Churches in Earliest Christianity.* Minneapolis: Augsburg Fortress, 2006.

Pervo, Richard. *The Acts of Paul: A New Translation with Introduction and Commentary.* Eugene, OR: Cascade, 2014.

Online resources

Ehrman, Bart. "The 'Anti-household' Paul: Thecla." Lecture, RLST 152: Introduction to the New Testament History and Literature. Open Yale Courses, Yale University, New Haven, CT. https://oyc.yale.edu/religious-studies/rlst-152/lecture-20.

NASSCAL (North American Society for the Study of Christian Apocryphal Literature) has produced an extensive bibliography on the *Acts of Paul and Thecla*. http://nasscal.com.

Chapter 6

Conclusion

In this conclusion to *Reclaiming Thecla*, we will share with you a few of our main points and leave you with some additional ideas and questions to consider in your own engagement with this fascinating second-century narrative. In particular, we wish to return to the question of how readers might reclaim Thecla today.

The chapters of this book were chosen to assist readers in navigating this narrative in its original context without losing sight of our own contexts today. We find that reading the *ATh* in light of the Greek romances and imagery from patron-broker-client relationships and in conversation with the theology of the Pastoral Epistles are fruitful ways of engaging this ancient narrative. There are many more areas we barely touched on and could have explored further, such as the relationship between the *ATh* and the other Apocryphal Acts, the development of the Thecla story in its various versions, the fifth-century *Life of Thecla*, and the cult of St. Thecla. We hope this book provides a useful entry point for deeper exploration.

Our study of the *ATh* in relation to scholarship on this text has resulted in a core conclusion: The *ATh* is a narrative synthesis of selected aspects of the Greek romance genre with emphasis on a particular ascetic understanding of the apostle Paul's teachings — his message of self-control — that connects to Paul specifically through a reading of 2 Timothy over against the views on female roles, decorum, and salvation in 1 Timothy 2:8–15. The *ATh* marshals an argument in narrative form for Thecla's ascetic way of being a female Christian itinerant teacher in which God, her divine patron, intervenes on her behalf during her trials and the apostle Paul

135

endorses her apostolic teaching ministry. The fervent support that Thecla receives from the crowd of matrons counters the claim that Thecla's refusal to marry is a threat to home and city and that she must die for shaming the imperial order in her public rebuttal of Alexander. The story ends with the statement that before Thecla died, she taught both men and women in her apostolic teaching ministry.

The Greek romances give the *ATh* its narrative form, as it borrows the pattern of lovers coming together, being pulled apart, facing trials, and coming back together. With everything but pirates, the adventure elements and tests of endurance would be familiar to the ancient audience. However, the audience would have expected the story to concern erotic love. The narrative style is the perfect template, therefore, to explore another way of looking at love in terms congenial to a Christian emphasis on agapic and familial love (*agape* and *storge*) rather than eros (romantic love).[1] Not only would the narrative form of the Greek romances have been familiar to the audience, but it also would have been a perfect Trojan horse to transform expectations into a story of agapic and familial love. Tryphaena loves Thecla like a daughter (29), and the main characters, the apostles Paul and Thecla, demonstrably have an agapic (25) and familial love (19) despite the ironic misunderstandings of Thamyris explicitly (13) and Theocleia implicitly (8), who think there is an erotic attachment. Learning about romantic love and endurance of hardship were central to the didactic function of the Greek romances; the *ATh*, however, transforms the romance template to provide examples of agapic and familial love in the midst of enduring difficult trials.

As a narrative in the style of the Greek romances, the *ATh* provides a fascinating foil to the Pastor's use of the epistle format in the PE. Greek romances culminate in the reunion and marriage of a hero and heroine, and the *ATh* ends with three paragraphs that tidy up the narrative in several ways. First, Thecla reunites with Paul and

---

[1] The *ATh* transforms the type of love in the Greek romances from *eros* to familial (*storge*) and agapic (19: *storge*; 25: *agapē*). Thamyris and Alexander have the eros type of love for Thecla (13: *phileō*; 26: *eraō*; 27: *phileō*).

receives the blessing of her apostolic teaching ministry (41). Second, Thecla returns home to Iconium at which point the narrative reaffirms that her devotion to Paul was entirely because he was the teacher who mediated the gospel message about the one who delivered her, Jesus, who is God (42). Lest anyone in the audience think that her devotion to Paul was erotic, an emphasis in the Greek romances, the narrative slams the door tightly shut on that idea. Third, the ending acts as a "Janus" passage, looking in both directions: The final paragraph (43) looks back to the beginning of the story regarding what motivated the plot when Thecla broke off her betrothal to Thamyris, who is declared dead. Thecla then tries to reconcile with her mother, Theocleia, testifying to her about rethinking the meaning of wealth and children, the loss of which Thecla had occasioned when she broke off her betrothal. Thecla's testimony relates to other early Christian narratives, including the Apocryphal Acts, in which family members, often husband and wife, were estranged when a main character embraces a form of the Christian message. Familial difficulties on account of becoming a Christian reflect Jesus's estrangement from family in Mark's Gospel (Mark 3:21, 31–34) and the hyperbolic saying "If anyone comes to me without hating his father and mother, wife and children, brothers and sisters, and even his own life, he cannot be my disciple" (Luke 14:26). The Book of Jonah ends with God's words to Jonah, which receive no response from the main character, so we never find out if Jonah had a change of heart about God's compassion for the Ninevites and its animals. So also in the *ATh*, we never learn whether Thecla's mother embraced the strange beliefs to which her daughter testifies. The story ends with that question unanswered. As a Janus passage, this final paragraph also looks forward beyond the narrative to Thecla's life of apostolic ministry "enlightening many."

A Greco-Roman audience would have related to the power dynamics in the *ATh* through a lens of patron-broker-client relations common to their culture. The patron-broker-client imagery that we see evident in the narrative, though not always explicitly spelled out, provides one way of understanding the theological dynamics concerning God's power to protect Thecla's honor, deliver her from immediate harm, and provide ultimate salvation. Like Paul, the great mediator of the message of salvation, Thecla acts as a powerful broker through prayer to transfer Falconilla to the place of the righteous. Also like Paul, she is a teacher who mediates the Christ movement's message within the story and to the audience. Moreover, she is a broker between Tryphaena and Paul, facilitating the distribution of her wealth for the "ministry to the poor" (41).

The *ATh* arises from the same culture as 1 Timothy and presupposes the same cultural ideas; both contain imagery drawn from the patronage system, including the *paterfamilias*. The *ATh*, however, communicates in narrative form a very different perspective on these matters from 1 Timothy. In Greco-Roman culture, the *paterfamilias* provides a structure where women are safe—as in a home—but the *ATh* emphasizes a theological point, namely, that God is the *paterfamilias* and everyone in the Christ movement is embedded within the household of God, who is Father. Crucially, the primary human *paterfamilias*, Paul, embraces Thecla's apostolic teaching ministry. Paul's role is complicated, however. Although he fails to protect Thecla from Alexander's advances and also disclaims the role of patron and *paterfamilias*, the *ATh* persuades the audience *through Paul's authority* to accept Thecla's apostolic teaching ministry to both men and women. While 1 Timothy also sees God as the ultimate *paterfamilias* of the community household, the Pastor persuades the audience *under the guise of Paul's authority* to emphasize women's subordinate roles in the community to the human *paterfamilias*.

In another sharp contrast, the Pastor in 1 Timothy 2:15 connects gender to salvation by insisting that women are saved through childbirth and socially constructed behavior with an emphasis on modesty. The *ATh* and the PE actually agree on salvation in two key ways: God desires the salvation of all, and those who are not Christian may ultimately find salvation. The latter view became increasingly unpopular through Augustine's influence, but these two texts indicate that it was a not uncommon idea in the second century. We argued in chapter 4 that the theological message around salvation concerns egalitarian access to the principles and teachings of the Christ movement. In contrast to the Pastor's perspective (1 Tim 2:15), salvation does not change based on one's gender in the *ATh*. That is, men and women are saved in precisely the same way, without the sense that salvation is linked to the control of women's decorum in assembly and acting modestly in subordination to the male head of house. It is probably not a coincidence that we never see Thecla in a community assembly in a home setting, the place where the Pastor seeks to control female behavior. Rather, the agapic love feast allusion occurs in a tomb (25), and when she is in a home she either teaches (39, 41) or prays (29, 41, 42).

The *ATh* is a narrative with specific implied rhetorical goals. In addition to the didactic function regarding agapic and familial love already noted, the *ATh* implicitly challenges its audience to accept God's salvation without gender qualifiers. Reading the *ATh* in light of ancient and modern discussions on sex and gender provides an opportunity for further reflection on important matters today regarding intersectional identities beyond the Thecla narrative. Since the *ATh* is part of a larger conversation on women's roles and salvation, reading the text today can be an opportunity to have a conversation that confronts traditions in biblical texts and beyond that either encourage subordination and exclusion or have been used in other harmful ways. As we indicate in the preface, a "hermeneutics of wholeness" prizes promoting the wholeness of everyone and should not aid or abet oppression.[2]

---

[2] St. Clair, "Womanist Biblical Interpretation," 59–60.

Appendix 1

Another Translation of the
Acts of Thecla[1]

III. Iconium

1 But, as Paul went up to Iconium, after his escape from Antioch, Demas and Hermogenes the blacksmith became his traveling companions. They were full of hypocrisy and flattered Paul as if they loved him. But Paul, looking only at the goodness of Christ, did them no harm. Rather, he loved them very much, so that to them all the words of the Lord are pleasant, as are those [words] of the instruction and interpretation concerning the birth and the resurrection of the Beloved. And he explained to them word by word the wonders of Christ, as that had been revealed to him: that it is from Mary and from David's seed that the Christ was born.

2 A man named Onesiphoros, having heard that Paul was going to arrive in Iconium, left with his sons Semaia and Zenon, as well as with his wife, Lectra, to meet Paul in order to receive him at their home. Titus, in fact, had described Paul's outward appearance, but he did not know him physically, only spiritually.

3 He walked up to the royal route that leads to Lystra, and he rested there, waiting for Paul. He observed the people who were arriving

---

[1] This translation by Vincent Skemp is from the French in "Actes de Paul," in *Écrits apocryphes chrétiens*, 1129–42. The French translation by W. Rordorf is in preparation for the critical edition of the Greek of the *Acts of Paul* to appear in Corpus Christianorum, Series Apocryphorum, edited by Rordorf and Jean-Daniel Kaestli.

based on Titus's description. Now, he saw Paul coming, a man of small size, bald head, bow-legged, sturdy, with eyebrows joined, with the nose slightly hooked, full of grace, and he had the countenance of an angel.

4 When he saw Onesiphoros, Paul smiled. And Onesiphoros said, "Hello, slave of the Blessed God!"

And Paul responded, "May grace be with you and with your house!"

But Demas and Hermogenes were jealous and displayed still more hypocrisy, so much that Demas said, "Do not the rest of us also belong to the Blessed God, so should you not greet us in the same way?"

Onesiphoros replied, "I do not see in you the fruit of righteousness, but if you are at all worthy, come, both of you, into my home, and rest yourselves!"

5 When Paul had entered Onesiphoros's home, there was great joy, knees were bent, bread was broken, they received the word of God concerning chastity and resurrection. Paul said:

Blessed are the pure of heart,
for they will see God.

Blessed are those who chastely guard their flesh,
for they will be temples of God.

Blessed are the chaste,
for God will speak with them.

Blessed are those who have renounced this world,
for they will please God.

Blessed are those who have wives as if they did not,
for they will be heirs of God.

Blessed are those who have awe of God,
for they will be angels.

6 Blessed are those who fear the words of God,

for they will be consoled.

Blessed are those who have received the wisdom of Jesus Christ,
for they will be called children of the Most High.

Blessed are those who have maintained baptism,
for they will find rest close to the Father and his beloved Son.

Blessed are those who have made room for the understanding of
Christ,
for they will be in the Light.

Blessed are those who, through love of God, have left behind the
appearance of the world,
for they will judge angels and will be taken up to the right of the
Father.

Blessed are the merciful,
for they will find mercy and they will not see the bitter Day of
Judgment.

Blessed are the bodies of virgins,
for they will be pleasing to God; they will not lose the reward of
their purity, for the word of the Father will become for them
beneficial work on the day of his Son, and they will find rest for
all eternity.

7 While Paul spoke thus in the presence of the assembly in the house
of Onesiphoros, Thecla, a virgin, whose mother was Theocleia, and
who was betrothed to a man by the name of Thamyris, situated
herself at the window of her house and listened in day and night to
the word of God proclaimed by Paul coming from the window next
door concerning purity, faith in Jesus Christ, and prayer. She did not
turn aside from the window, but at the height of joy, she was
overcome by faith. Moreover, as she saw many women enter close
to Paul, she desired that she also be considered worthy of being face
to face with him and to listen to the word of Christ, but she had not
yet seen Paul's features, but had only listened to his eloquence.

8 However, since she would not leave the window, her mother sent for Thamyris. He came full of joy, thinking that he had already received the girl in marriage. Therefore, Thamyris said to Theocleia, "Where is my Thecla that I may see her?"

And Theocleia responded to him: "I have to let you know something new, Thamyris. It has been in fact three days and three nights; Thecla hasn't left the window, neither to eat nor to drink, but her gaze is fixed as if on account of a joyousness. She is so attached to a strange man who teaches deceitful, ambiguous, and frivolous words that I am surprised to see the virgin's great modesty troubled in a manner so painful.

9 "Thamyris, this man has upset the city of the Iconians and your Thecla also. In fact, all the women and young people go to him, and he teaches them that they must believe in only one God and live in purity. In turn, my daughter is also immobilized by his words as by a spider at the window; she is under the control of a new desire and a strange passion. She is suspended by his words and has succumbed. But go to her and speak with her, for it is to you that she should be united."

10 Thamyris approached Thecla, at the same time full of love for her and full of fear of her ecstasy, and said, "Thecla, my betrothed, why do you remain seated thus? And what passion has sway over you that it makes you act so unusually? Turn yourself toward your Thamyris and show shame!"

At his side, her mother also said the same thing: "Thecla, my child, why do you remain seated thus, looking below, and scarcely responding, but dumbstruck?"

And everyone in the house wept copiously: Thamyris, because he had lost his woman; Theocleia, her child; and the young slaves, their mistress. Great was thus the disturbance and grief in the house. And in spite of all this, Thecla did not turn back, but maintained all her attention on the word of Paul.

11 Then Thamyris, leaping up, went out into the street and began to observe those who were going to Paul and those who were leaving from there. And he saw two men who were violently quarreling, and he said to them: "Men, tell me who you are and who is this seducer who remains with you inside, who beguiles the sensibilities of young people and virgins in order that they don't marry but remain as they are? I promise to give you a lot of money if you tell me about him. For I am one of the leading men of the city."

12 And Demas and Hermogenes responded to him: "Who he is, we do not know, but he causes the young women and virgins to set aside the men by saying, 'There will be no resurrection for you unless you remain chaste and do not sully the flesh but keep pure.'"

13 Thamyris said to them: "Come, men, let's go to my home and rest there!" And they departed for a sumptuous meal, with much wine, a great display of opulence, and a splendid table. And Thamyris, who loved Thecla and wanted to have her for his wife, made them drink. And during the meal Thamyris said: "Men, tell me what his teaching is so that I too may know about it. For I am in great pain on account of Thecla because she loves this stranger so much and I am deprived of marriage."

14 But Demas and Hermogenes spoke in unison: "Thamyris, escort him to Governor Castellius and accuse him of seducing the crowds by teaching Christian frivolity. In this way, he will be put to death, and as for you, you will have Thecla for your wife. And we will teach you that this resurrection, which this man says is future, has already happened through the children that we have and that we are resurrected by acknowledging the true God."

15 When he heard this, Thamyris was filled with jealousy and rage; at dawn he got up and went to the house of Onesiphoros in the company of the magistrates, functionaries, and a rather large crowd armed with sticks. He said to Paul, "You seduced the city of the

Iconians and my betrothed so that she no longer wants to marry me. We are going in front of Governor Castellius!"

And the entire crowd said, "Take away the magician because he has seduced all our women!"

16 And Thamyris, standing before the tribunal, said with a loud voice: "Proconsul, we do not know from where this man comes who hinders the virgins from marrying; let him say before you why he is teaching that."

But Demas and Hermogenes said to Thamyris, "Denounce him as Christian and he will perish immediately."

But the proconsul made his decision, addressed Paul, and said to him, "Who are you and what do you teach? For this is not a small matter that they accuse you of."

17 And Paul raised his voice saying, "Since today I have to give an account of my teaching, listen, proconsul. The living God, the God of chastisement, the God who is self-sufficient but who desires the salvation of humankind, sent me to wrest them from corruption, impurity, every desire, and death so that they might no longer sin; it is because God sent his own Son that I proclaim and I teach that people have in him their hope, in him who alone had pity on the world gone astray, so that people no longer fall under the blow of judgment but receive faith and fear of God, knowledge of sanctity and love of truth. If then I teach that which has been revealed to me by God, in what way am I wrong, proconsul?" After having heard these words, the proconsul ordered that Paul be chained and brought to prison until he had the time to understand more thoroughly.

18 But Thecla, at night, removed her bracelets and gave them to the doorkeeper; the latter opened the door for her, and she went into the prison. She gave the prison guard a silver mirror, and she entered near Paul. She sat at his feet and listened to the wonders of God. And Paul had fear of nothing but conducted himself with the assurance of God. Her faith was growing in her, and she kissed his chains.

19 While her family was looking for Thecla, and Thamyris, believing her lost, ran into the street, one of the slaves, friend of the doorman, declared that she had gone out at night. Then they questioned the doorman, who told them that she had proclaimed, "I am going to the side of the stranger in prison." They went, based on what the slave had told them, and found her prisoner with him in love, so to speak. And going out from there, they brought in the crowd and disclosed to the governor what had happened.

20 He then ordered that Paul be brought before the tribunal. But Thecla rolled around on the ground at the place where Paul, seated in prison, had taught. And the governor ordered her also to be brought before the tribunal. Then she departed with joy in cheerfulness.

When Paul was brought from the prison, the crowd shouted out stronger, "He is a magician! Kill him!"

However, the proconsul heard Paul with pleasure speak of his works; having taken counsel, he had Thecla called forth and said to her, "Why do you not marry Thamyris according to Iconian law?" But she remained there, her eyes fixed on Paul.

Since she did not respond, Theocleia, her mother, exclaimed, "Burn this criminal! Burn this enemy of marriage in the middle of the theater so that all the women instructed by this man are terror-stricken!"

21 The governor suffered greatly. He had Paul flogged and banished from the city, and he condemned Thecla to be burned. Immediately, the governor rose and went to the theater. The entire crowd went out to this imposed spectacle. But just as a lamb in the desert looks all about to see the shepherd, so Thecla looked all about to see Paul. And while she examined the crowd, she saw the Lord seated, in the guise of Paul, and she said, "Paul has come to observe me as if I were without endurance." And she turned her eyes to him and stared at him, but he went up to heaven.

22 Meanwhile, the young people and young girls carried wood to burn Thecla. When she was introduced naked, the governor wept, and he admired the strength that was in her. The executioners erected the wood and ordered her to mount the pyre. She, in forming the image of the cross, mounted the wood. They lit the fire. Even though a high flame burned, the fire did not touch her. In fact, God had pity and aroused an underground noise, and from above, a cloud filled with rain and hail spread its shadow; a huge amount of water poured out so that many were put in danger and died, but the fire was extinguished and Thecla was saved.

23 Paul was fasting with Onesiphoros, his wife, and children in an open tomb on the road that goes from Iconium to Daphne. As they had spent several days in fasting, the children said to Paul, "We are hungry." But they had nothing with which to buy bread; in fact, Onesiphoros had abandoned material possessions and was following Paul with his entire family. Paul then removed his garment and said, "Come, child, purchase some bread and bring it back!"

While the child was purchasing, he saw Thecla, the neighbor; he was amazed and said, "Thecla, where are you going?"

She responded, "I am looking for Paul after having escaped the fire."

The child said, "Come. I will lead you to him, but he moans about your situation, and he prays and fasts for six days already."

24 When she arrived at the tomb, she saw that Paul was on his knees and praying, saying, "Holy Father, Jesus Christ, may fire not touch Thecla, but help her, for she is yours."

She, standing behind him, cried out and said, "Father, you who made heaven and earth, Father of your holy Child, I praise you because you have saved me so that I may see Paul."

And Paul got up, saw her, and said, "God, you who know our hearts, Father of Jesus Christ, I praise you for having so quickly granted my request and listened to me."

25 And inside the tomb there was great conveyance of affection. Paul, Onesiphoros, and all the others were joyful. They had five loaves of bread, vegetables, and water. And they were gladdened by the holy works of Christ. And Thecla said to Paul, "I am going to cut my hair, and I will follow you wherever you go."

But he responded to her, "The time is wicked, and you are beautiful. And I fear that another trial, worse than the first, may come upon you, and that you may not be able to endure it, but that in it you weaken."

And Thecla said, "Only give me the seal in Christ, and no trial will overtake me."

And Paul said to Thecla, "Be patient, and you will receive the water."

And Paul sent Onesiphoros and his entire family back to Iconium; and so he took Thecla and entered Antioch.

IV. Antioch[2]

1 (26) But at the moment when they were entering there, a Syrian named Alexander—a citizen of high standing among the Antiochenes, very active in that city in the office that he exercised— saw Thecla and fell in love with her. He strove to ensure Paul's complacency with money and gifts.

But Paul said, "I do not know this woman in the way that you say; she does not belong to me." And the man, who had great power, embraced Thecla in the street. Now, she did not tolerate it, but she sought out Paul.

She began to cry and say bitterly, "Do not do violence to the stranger! Do not do violence to the slave of God! I am among the leading women of the Iconians, and it is because I have refused to marry Thamyris that I was driven from that city." Then, taking hold of Alexander, she tore his mantle, removed the wreath from his head, and exposed him to public scorn.

---

[2] The main numbering system in this section, provided in bold, follows the convention that the Antioch segment is chapter 4 of the *Acts of Paul*, thus restarting the numbering. The numbers in parentheses correspond to the numbering convention of the translation provided in chapter 1 of this volume.

2 (27) Then he, at the same time loving her and ashamed at what had happened to him, brought her to the governor. Since she had confessed to having done it, the latter condemned her to be thrown to the beasts. It happened that Alexander organized the animal games. The women of the city were seized with indignation and cried out before the tribunal: "Criminal judgment! Impious judgment!" Thecla asked the governor that she be able to remain pure until the moment when she would have to fight against the beasts. And she was confined to the care of a wealthy woman named Tryphaena, of royal family, whose daughter had died, and this woman was the consolation of Thecla.

3 (28) When the parade of beasts began, Thecla was attacked by a ferocious lion, and Queen Tryphaena followed her. But the lioness on which Thecla was mounted licked her feet, and the whole crowd was upset. The grounds of conviction listed on the inscription was this: "sacrilege." The women with their children cried out, saying, "Impieties are committed in this city."

And, after the procession, Tryphaena again took Thecla to her home. Her deceased daughter appeared to her in a dream, saying, "Mother, you will take Thecla, the stranger, the abandoned one, in my place so that she may pray for me and I may be transferred to the abode of the righteous."

4 (29) After the parade, Tryphaena then welcomed Thecla into her home. On the one hand, she was grieved because the next day Thecla was to battle the beasts; on the other hand, she loved her daughter Falconilla. And she said, "Thecla, my second child, behold, pray for my daughter, so that she may live. It is in fact this that I have seen in a dream."

And Thecla, without delay, lifted up her voice and said, "God of the heavens, Son of the Most High, grant her, according to her wish, that her daughter Falconilla live for eternity." And having heard these things, Tryphaena grieved thinking of such beauty that was to be thrown to the beasts.

5 (30) When dawn arose, Alexander went to take Thecla — for he was the one who organized the animal games — and said to Tryphaena, "The governor is seated and the crowd clamors against us. Let me lead the condemned to the beasts."

But Tryphaena began shouting to the point of making Alexander flee, saying, "Falconilla, this is a second mourning that has happened to my house! And nobody will help me: neither child, since she died, nor kin, since I am a widow. God of Thecla, my child, help her!"

6 (31) Then the governor sent soldiers to take Thecla away. However, Tryphaena did not abandon her, but taking her herself by the hand, she lead her in, saying, "My daughter Falconilla, I took her to the grave, and you, Thecla, I will take you to fight against the beasts."

Thecla then wept bitterly, groaned to the Lord, saying, "Lord, God, in whom I believe, at whose side I took refuge, who extracted me from the fire, reward Tryphaena for having had pity on your slave and for having preserved my purity!"

7 (32) There was then commotion, loud noise of beasts and cries of the people and the women seated together. The people said, "Bring the sacrilegious one!" whereas the women were saying, "May the city perish for this injustice! Kill us all, proconsul! Hateful spectacle! Criminal sentence!"

8 (33) As for Thecla, she was taken from the hands of Tryphaena, they stripped her, a loin cloth was put on her, and they threw her into the stadium. The lions and bears were released against her. Then the ferocious lioness, rushing up, lay down at her feet. And the crowd of women gasped. And a bear rushed at Thecla, but the lioness went to meet the bear and tore it to pieces. In turn, a lion, trained to devour humans and [who] belonged to Alexander, rushed at Thecla; but the lioness fought against the lion in a mêlée and perished with him. And the women were even more grief stricken because the lioness who had come to Thecla's aid had also died.

9 (34) Then they released numerous wild beasts, while Thecla, standing, stretched out her hands and prayed. When she had finished her prayer, she turned, saw a big pit full of water and said, "Now is the moment to receive the bath." And she threw herself in: "In the name of Jesus Christ, I am baptized on my last day."

Seeing this, the women and all the people cried out by saying: "Don't throw yourself into the water!" It was then that even the governor shed tears at the idea that the seals were going to devour such beauty. She then threw herself into the water in the name of Jesus Christ, but the seals, seeing the sudden flash of lightning, floated to the surface, dead. And a cloud of fire spread around Thecla so that the beasts did not touch her and her nakedness escaped their notice.

10 (35) As the other ferocious beasts were released, the women uttered cries; and each threw aromatic spices—some nard, others cassia, others cardamom, so that there was a mass of fragrances. Then all the animals, slackened as if overpowered by sleep, did not touch her, so that Alexander said to the governor, "I have very ferocious bulls; fasten the condemned to them!"

With a somber air, the governor consented to it: "Do what you want!" Then they fastened Thecla by the feet in the midst of the bulls, and they applied to their genitals irons heated by fire so that, excited to the highest degree, they might kill her. They indeed began to spring up, but the flame extending all around burned the ropes, and Thecla was found as if she had not been bound.

11 (36) However, Tryphaena, standing near the arena toward the first seats, fainted, so that her slaves said, "Queen Tryphaena is dead!" The governor ordered that they stop the spectacle, and the entire city was in anguish.

Alexander, throwing himself at the feet of the governor, said, "Have pity on me and this city and release the condemned, lest the city also perish! For if the emperor learns of these things, he will no doubt destroy the city because his relative Queen Tryphaena died by the best seats."

12 (37) Then the governor had Thecla led from the midst of the beasts and said to her, "Who are you? And what protection surrounds you so that not a single beast touched you?"

Thecla responded, "I am the slave of the living God. The protection that encircles me, it is to have believed in the one whom God put his good pleasure, his Son. It is by him that not a single beast has touched me. He alone in fact is the pillar of salvation, the foundation of immortal life; for he becomes refuge for those who are tossed by the storm, rest for the afflicted, shelter for the desperate; in a word, those who have not believed in him shall not live but will die for eternity."

13 (38) At these words, the governor ordered that clothing be brought and said, "Put on these garments, Thecla!"

But she said, "The one who clothed me when I was naked in the midst of the wild beasts, that one, on the Day of Judgment, will clothe me for salvation." And having taken the clothing, she covered herself with them.

And the governor immediately issued a decree, saying, "I release you, Thecla, slave of God, Thecla, adorer of God."

Then the women cried out in a strong voice and, as one mouth, praised God by saying, "There is only one God, the one who saved Thecla," so that the city was unsettled by this clamor,

14 (39) and so that Tryphaena, after having learned the good news, went to meet Thecla with the crowd, embraced her, and said, "Now I believe that the dead may rise again; now I believe that my daughter lives. Thecla, my child, enter into my house, that I may inscribe all my goods to your name!" Thecla entered then with Tryphaena and rested in her house for eight days, teaching her the word of God so that Tryphaena believed, as well as most of her slaves, and joy was great in the house.

15 (40) But Thecla ardently desired to see Paul again and had envoys search for him everywhere; they informed her that he was in Myra. She then took some young male slaves and young female slaves, girded her loins, and, arranging her tunic to make a garment in the style of the men, she went to Myra. She found Paul expounding the word of God and drew near him. However, he was amazed upon seeing her and the crowd that was accompanying her, thinking that some other trial had happened to Thecla. But she, having come to understand him, said to him, "I have received baptism, Paul. In fact, he who worked with you for the good news has also worked with me so that I am baptized."

16 (41) Paul took her with him and led her away into the house of Hermias. Then Thecla recounted to Paul everything that had happened to her so that Paul was greatly surprised by it, and those listening were strengthened and prayed for Tryphaena. And Thecla, standing up, said to Paul, "I am going to Iconium."

Paul responded to her: "Go and teach the word of God." For her part, Tryphaena sent a great deal of clothing and gold to Thecla so that she left much to Paul for service to the poor.

17 (42) Then Thecla went to Iconium. And she entered into the house of Onesiphoros, threw herself to the ground at the place where Paul also had taught and wept by saying, "O our God, God of this house where the Light shined for me, Christ Jesus, Son of God, my help in prison, my help before governors, my help in the fire, my help among the beasts, you are the God to whom belong the glory forever, Amen."

18 (43) And she found Thamyris dead, but her mother was living; and she sent for the latter and said to her, "Theocleia, my mother, are you able to believe that a Lord lives in heaven? In fact, if you desire riches, God will give them to you through me; if you desire your child, I am close to you." And rendering this testimony, she left for Seleucia, and having enlightened many people with the word of God, she fell asleep in a good sleep.

Appendix 2

Homer's *Odyssey* and Euripides's *Hippolytus*

Readers of the Greek romances who are familiar with Homer's *Odyssey* will see similarities between themes in the Greek romances and the *Odyssey*, the story of Odysseus's many trials as he strives to return to his wife Penelope and son Telemachus, who do not know whether he still lives. Penelope is being courted by over one hundred suitors who conspire to kill their son Telemachus. The Greek romances derive themes from Homer's *Odyssey*, including suffering and endurance of trials in an effort to return home (*nostos*), suitors who endanger the couple's reunion, and the importance of *xenia*, sacred hospitality toward guests. The backstory of the Homeric epics, viz. Alexander (Paris) abducts Helen, which is the cause of conflict between two men and two armies, plays out in *Callirhoe* when the title character is abducted and becomes the object of conflict between Chaereas and Dionysius. *Callirhoe* three times explicitly alludes to Callirhoe as Helen (2.6; 5.2; 5.5).[1] Whereas the Greek romances allude to the *Iliad* and the *Odyssey* and sometimes quote Homer (e.g., *Call* 1.1 // *Od* 4.704), any corollaries between the *ATh* and Homer derive from the *ATh*'s association with the Greek romances, which is to say that the *ATh* is a step removed from the Homeric story. In contrast to the romances, the *ATh* never quotes Homer or alludes to Thecla as Helen-like or Penelope-like. A possible faint Homeric allusion may be the choice of the name Alexander for the man who accosts Thecla.

---

[1] On the relation between Homer and the Greek romances, see Graverini, "From the Epic to the Novelistic Hero"; Zanetto, "Greek Novel and Greek Archaic Literature."

A century ago, Ludwig Radermacher read the Thecla stories—both the *A Th* in its various forms and the fifth century *Life and Miracles*—as literature rather than try to find an historical nucleus to the legends about her. Radermacher noted similarities between Thecla and mythological figures (e.g., nymphs, Athena, Artemis) and stories, including Euripides's *Hippolytus*.[2] The destroying bull in the Euripidean tragedy parallels to some extent the bulls used to torture Thecla (*A Th* 35), and the two works share a concern for the problem of desire and endurance of suffering. Radermacher was among those who pointed out that the fifth century *Life and Miracles* rewrites the ending of the *A Th* so that she experiences a disappearance similar to that of Hippolytus (cf. *Life* 28.5–10).[3]

The plot of *Hippolytus* revolves around Phaedra's divinely inflicted infatuation with the chaste Hippolytus, her stepson. When Hippolytus rejects her advances, Phaedra kills herself in despair. Hippolytus's father, Theseus, wrongly blames his son for his wife's death and curses him, resulting in Hippolytus's destruction by a divinely sent bull. With the bull in chase, Hippolytus becomes entangled in his horses' reins and disappears. The tragedy explores the power of erotic infatuation and the importance of moderation vis-à-vis the extreme perspectives of the main characters: Phaedra's desire, Hippolytus's chastity, and Theseus's intransigence. The slave nurse initially counsels Phaedra to endure her suffering, cease from excessive desire, and practice moderation; the nurse, however, changes course and tries to persuade Phaedra to act on her passion.

Although the *A Th* nowhere quotes *Hippolytus*, there are intriguing thematic connections between the two works, and undoubtedly the later *Life and Miracles* is indebted to the Hippolytus story for the disappearance motif. It is plausible that the bulls used to torture Thecla (*A Th* 35) may have evoked for a Greco-Roman audience the destroying bull of the Hippolytus myth.[4]

---

[2] Radermacher, *Hippolytos und Thekla*, 4–10, 51–69, 91–92, 117–26. He addresses (8–10) that there are multiple allusions to and variations of the Hippolytus myth.

[3] Radermacher, *Hippolytos und Thekla*, 60–61, 117–20.

[4] Rordorf, *Écrits apocryphes chrétiens*, 1140, n. IV, 10.

Reading the *ATh* in the light of parallels with Greco-Roman mythology, an approach we employ with the spider imagery at *ATh* 9,[5] can facilitate locating analogs available to a Greco-Roman audience but unfamiliar to modern readers. However, we can more firmly establish *An Ephesian Tale* and specific New Testament texts as clear intertexts with the *ATh*.

In sum, an ancient audience may have associated the *ATh* with broad plot points and thematic archetypes present in the Homeric narrative, as the Homeric epics are the primary model for the Greek romances, but the *ATh* is a step removed from Homer. Possible allusions to the Hippolytus story in the *ATh* are similarly faint but become stronger in the *Life and Miracles* with the disappearance motif. We can establish with confidence the primary intertexts for the *ATh*, the Greek romance *An Ephesian Tale*, and certain New Testament texts.

---

[5] See the discussion of the spider imagery on pp. 100–101.

Bibliography

Sources and Translations

"Actes de Paul." In *Écrits apocryphes chrétiens*, edited by François Bovon and Pierre Geoltrain, translated by Willy Rordorf with Pierre Cherix and Rudolphe Kasser, 1115–77. Bibliothèque de la Pléiade. Saint Herblain: Gallimard, 1997.

"Acts of Paul and Thecla." [In Greek]. In *Acta apostolorum apocrypha*, edited by Richard A. Lipsius and Maximilien Bonnet, 235–72. Vol. 1. Leipzig: Mendelssohn, 1891–1903. Reprint, Hildescheim, Germany: G. Olms, 1959.

Collected Ancient Greek Novels. Edited by B. P. Reardon. Translated by Graham Anderson. Berkeley: University of California, 1989.

An Ephesian Tale. In *Two Novels from Ancient Greece: Chariton's Callirhoe and Xenophon of Ephesos' An Ephesian Story*, translated by Stephen M. Trzaskoma, 125–69. Indianapolis: Hackett Publishing, 2010.

Greek Fiction: Callirhoe, Daphnis and Chloe, Letters of Chion. Edited by Helen Morales. Translated by Rosanna Omitowoju, Phiroze Vasunia, and John Penwill. London: Penguin Classics, 2011.

Kaestli, Jean-Daniel, and Gérard Poupon. "Les *Actes de Paul et Thècle* latins: Édition de la version A et de sa réécriture dans le manuscrit de Dublin, Trinity College, 174." *Apocrypha* 27 (2016): 9–110.

Secondary Literature

Ahmed, Sara. *Living a Feminist Life*. Durham, NC: Duke University Press, 2017.

Albrecht, Ruth. *Das Leben der heiligen Makrina auf dem Hintergrund der Thekla-traditionen: Studien zu den Ursprüngen des weiblichen Mönchtums im 4. Jahrhundert in Kleinasien*. Göttingen: Vandenhoeck & Ruprecht, 1986.

Andrious, Rosie. *Saint Thecla: Body Politic and Masculine Rhetoric*. London: T&T Clark, 2020.

159

Anzaldúa, Gloria. *Borderlands/La Frontera: The New Mestiza*. 3rd ed. San Francisco: Aunt Lute Books, 2007.

————. "Now let us shift . . . the path of conocimiento . . . inner work, public act." In *This Bridge We Call Home: Radical Visions of Transformation*, edited by Gloria E. Anzaldúa and AnaLouise Keating, 540–78. New York: Routledge, 2002.

Appel, Andrea. "Möglichkeiten und Grenzen für ein Ampt der Frau in frühchristlichen Gemeinden am beispiel der Pastoralbriefe und der Thekla-Akten." In *Frauen in der Geschichte*, edited by Werner Affeldt and Annette Kuhn, 7.244–56. Düsseldorf: Pädagogischer Verlag Schwann, 1986.

Arjava, Antti. "Paternal Power in Late Antiquity." *Journal of Roman Studies* 88 (1998): 147–65.

Aubin, Melissa, "Reversing Romance? The Acts of Thecla and the Ancient Novel." In *Ancient Fiction and Early Christian Narrative*, edited by R. Hock, J. B. Chance, and J. Perkens, 257–72. Atlanta: Society of Biblical Literature, 1998.

Ault, Bradley A. "Living in the Classical *Polis*: The Greek House as Microcosm." *Classical World* 93, no. 5 (May–June 2000): 483–96.

Aune, David. "Passions in the Pauline Epistles: the Current State of Research." In *Passions and Moral Progress in Greco-Roman Thought*, ed. John T. Fitzgerald, 221–37. London: Routledge, 2008.

Aymer, Margaret P. "Hailstorms and Fireballs: Redaction, World Creation and Resistance in the Acts of Paul and Thecla." *Semeia* 79 (1997): 45–62.

Baker, Courtney R. *Humane Insight: Looking at Images of African American Suffering and Death*. New Black Studies Series. Urbana, IL: University of Illinois Press, 2015.

Barrier, Jeremy. *The Acts of Paul: A Critical Introduction and Commentary*. Wissenschaftliche Untersuchungen zum Neuen Testament 270. Tübingen: Mohr Siebeck, 2009.

Bassler, Jouette M. *1 Timothy, 2 Timothy, Titus*. Abingdon New Testament Commentaries. Nashville: Abingdon Press, 1996.

————. "A Fresh Look at 1 Tim 5:3–16." *Journal of Biblical Literature* 103, no. 1 (March 1984): 23–41.

————. *Navigating Paul: An Introduction to Key Theological Concepts*. Louisville: Westminster John Knox, 2002.

Bauckham, Richard. "The Acts of Paul as a Sequel to Acts." In *The Book of Acts in its Ancient Literary Setting*, edited by Bruce Winter and Andrew Clarke, 105–52. The Book of Acts in its First Century Setting, vol. 1. Grand Rapids: Eerdmans, 1993.

Betz, Monika. "Die Betörenden Worte des fremden Mannes: Zur Funktion der Paulusbeschreibung in den Theklaakten." *New Testament Studies* 53, no. 1 (2007): 130–45.

Bollók, János. "The Description of Paul in the Acta Pauli." In *The Apocryphal Acts of Paul and Thecla*, edited by Jan N. Bremmer, 1–15. Kampen, Netherlands: Kok Pharos, 1996.

Blount, Brian. *Then the Whisper Put on Flesh: New Testament Ethics in an African American Context*. Nashville: Abingdon Press, 2001.

Boughton, Lynne C. "From Pious Legend to Feminist Fantasy: Distinguishing Hagiographical License from Apostolic Practice in the *Acts of Paul/Acts of Thecla*." *Journal of Religion* 71, no. 3 (July 1991): 362–83.

Bowie, Ewen, "The Ancient Readers of the Greek Novels." In *The Novel in the Ancient World*, edited by Gareth Schmeling, 87–106. Rev. ed. Leiden: Brill, 2003.

Boyarin, Daniel. *A Radical Jew: Paul and the Politics of Identity*. Berkeley: University of California Press, 1994.

Braun, Willi. "Physiotherapy of Femininity in the Acts of Thecla." In *Text and Artifact in the Religions of Mediterranean Antiquity: Essays in Honor of Peter Richardson*, edited by Stephen Wilson and Michel Desjardins, 209–30. Studies in Christianity and Judaism 9. Waterloo, Ontario: Wilfrid Laurier University, 2000.

Bremmer, Jan, N., ed. *The Apocryphal Acts of Paul and Thecla*. Kampen, Netherlands: Kok Pharos, 1996.

———. "Conversion in the Oldest Apocryphal Acts." In *Maidens, Magic and Martyrs in Early Christianity*, 181–96. Tübingen: Mohr Siebeck, 2017.

———. *Maidens, Magic and Martyrs in Early Christianity*. Wissenschaftliche Untersuchungen zum Neuen Testament 379. Tübingen: Mohr Siebeck, 2017.

Brown, Peter. *The Body and Society: Men, Women, and Sexual Renunciation in Early Christianity*. New York: Columbia University Press, 1988.

Butler, Judith. *Gender Trouble: Feminism and the Subversion of Identity*. New York: Routledge Classics, 1990.

Burrus, Virginia. *Chastity as Autonomy: Women in the Stories of Apocryphal Acts.* Studies in Women and Religion, vol. 23. Lewiston, NY: Edwin Mellen, 1986.

Byrd, Jodi A. *The Transit of Empire: Indigenous Critiques of Colonialism.* First Peoples: New Directions in Indigenous Studies. Minneapolis: University of Minnesota Press, 2011.

Calef, Susan A. "Thecla 'Tried and True' and the Inversion of Romance." In *A Feminist Companion to the New Testament Apocrypha,* edited by Amy-Jill Levine with Maria Mayo Robbins, 163–85. Cleveland: The Pilgrim Press, 2006.

Callon, Callie. *Reading Bodies: Physiognomy as a Strategy of Persuasion in Early Christian Discourse.* Library of New Testament Studies 579. London: T&T Clark, 2019.

Camp, Claudia V. "Wise and Strange: An Interpretation of the Female Imagery in Proverbs in Light of Trickster Mythology." In *A Feminist Companion to Wisdom Literature,* edited by Athalya Brenner, 131–56. Feminist Companion to the Bible 9. Sheffield: Sheffield Academic Press, 1995.

Campbell, Ken M., ed. *Marriage and Family in the Biblical World.* Downers Grove, IL: InterVarsity Press, 2003.

Carter, Warren. *The Roman Empire and the New Testament: An Essential Guide.* Nashville: Abingdon, 2006.

Chan, Chi Wai. "The Ultimate Trickster in the Story of Tamar from a Feminist Perspective." *Feminist Theology* 24, no. 1 (2015): 93–101.

Cohick, Lynn H. "Mothers, Martyrs, and Manly Courage: The Female Martyr in 2 Maccabees, 4 Maccabees, and the Acts of Thecla." In *A Most Reliable Witness: Essays in Honor of Ross Shepard Kraemer,* edited by Susan Ashbrook Harvey, Nathaniel DeRosiers, Shira L. Landers, Jacqueline Pastis, and Daniel Ullicci, 123–31. Providence: Brown University Press, 2015.

Coleman, Monica A. *Making a Way out of No Way: A Womanist Theology.* Minneapolis: Fortress Press, 2008.

Collins, Raymond F. *1 & 2 Timothy and Titus: A Commentary.* Louisville: Westminster John Knox, 2002.

———. *First Corinthians.* Edited by Daniel J. Harrington. Sacra Pagina 7. Collegeville, MN: The Liturgical Press, 1999.

Cone, James. *The Cross and the Lynching Tree*. Maryknoll, NY: Orbis Books, 2011.

Cooper, Kate. *The Virgin and the Bride: Idealized Womanhood in Late Antiquity*. Cambridge, MA: Harvard University Press, 1996.

———. *Band of Angels: The Forgotten World of Early Christian Women*. New York: The Overlook Press, 2013.

Dagron, Gilbert. *Vie et Miracles de Sainte Thècle: Texte grec, traduction et commentaire par Gilbert Dagron, avec la collaboration de Marie Dupré La Tour*. Brussels: Société des Bollandistes, 1978.

D'Angelo, Mary Rose. "'Knowing How to Preside over His Own Household': Imperial Masculinity and Christian Asceticism in the Pastorals, Hermas, and Luke-Acts." In *New Testament Masculinities*, edited by Stephen D. Moore and Janice Capel Anderson, 265–95. Semeia 45. Atlanta: Society of Biblical Literature, 2004.

Davies, Stevan L. *The Revolt of the Widows: The Social World of the Apocryphal Acts*. Dublin: Bardic Press, 1980 and 2012.

Davis, Angela, ed. *Policing the Black Man: Arrest, Prosecution and Imprisonment*. New York: Vintage Books, 2018.

Davis, Stephen J. "A 'Pauline' Defense of Women's Right to Baptize? Intertextuality and Apostolic Authority in the Acts of Paul." *Journal of Early Christian Studies* 8, no. 3 (2000): 453–59.

———. *The Cult of St. Thecla: A Tradition of Women's Piety in Late Antiquity*. Oxford: Oxford University Press, 2001.

den Dulk, Matthijs. "I Permit No Woman to Teach except for Thecla: The Curious Case of the Pastoral Epistles and the *Acts of Paul* Reconsidered." *Novum Testamentum* 54, no. 2 (2012): 176–203.

deSilva, David A. "Patronage." In *Dictionary of New Testament Background*, edited by Craig A. Evans and Stanley E. Porter, 766–71. Downers Grove, IL: Intervarsity Press, 2000.

———. *Honor, Patronage, Kinship and Purity: Unlocking the New Testament Culture*. Downers Grove, IL: InterVarsity Press, 2000.

Douglas, Kelly Brown. *Stand Your Ground: Black Bodies and the Justice of God*. Maryknoll, NY: Orbis Books, 2015.

Du Mez, Kristin Kobes. *Jesus and John Wayne: How White Evangelicals Corrupted a Faith and Fractured a Nation*. New York: Liveright, 2020.

Dunn, Peter. "The Acts of Paul and the Pauline Legacy in the Second Century." PhD diss., Cambridge University, 1996.

———. "Women's Liberation: The Acts of Paul, and Other Apocryphal Acts of the Apostles: A Review of Some Recent Interpreters." *Apocrypha* 4 (1993): 245–81.

Dunning, Benjamin H. *Specters of Paul: Sexual Difference in Early Christian Thought.* Philadelphia: University of Pennsylvania Press, 2011.

Edsall, Benjamin. "(Not) Baptizing Thecla: Early Interpretive Efforts in 1 Cor 1:17." *Vigiliae Christianae* 71, no. 3 (2017): 235–60.

Egger, Brigitte. "The Role of Women in the Greek Novel: Women as Heroine and Reader." In *Oxford Readings in the Greek Novel*, edited by Simon Swain, 108–36. Oxford: Oxford University Press, 1999.

Ehrman, Bart. "The 'Anti-household' Paul: Thecla." Lecture, RLST 152: Introduction to the New Testament History and Literature, Open Yale Courses, Yale University, New Haven, CT. https://oyc.yale.edu/religious-studies/rlst-152/lecture-20.

Elenes, C. Alejandra. "Nepantla, Spiritual Activism, New Tribalism: Chicana Feminist Transformative Pedagogies and Social Justice Education." *Journal of Latino/Latin American Studies* 5, no. 3 (2013): 132–41.

Elliott, Colin. *Economic Theory and the Roman Monetary Economy.* Cambridge, UK: Cambridge University Press, 2020.

Elliott, John H. "Patronage and Clientage." In *The Social Sciences and New Testament Interpretation*, edited by Richard L. Rohrbaugh, 144–56. Grand Rapids, MI: Baker Academic, 1996.

———. *1 Peter: A New Translation with Introduction and Commentary.* New York: Doubleday, 2000.

Esch-Wermeling, Elisabeth. *Thekla — Paulusschülerin wider Willen? Strategien der Leserlenkung in den Theklaakten.* Neutestamentliche Abhandlungen 53. Münster: Aschendorff, 2008.

Evans-Grubbs, Judith. "Abduction Marriage in Antiquity: A Law of Constantine (CTh IX.24.I) and Its Social Context." *Journal of Roman Studies* 79 (1989): 59–83.

Eyl, Jennifer. "Why Thekla Does Not See Paul: Visual Perception and the Displacement of Eros in the Acts of Paul and Thekla." In *The Ancient Novel and Early Christian and Jewish Narrative: Fictional Intersections*, edited by

Marília Futre Pinheiro, Judith Perkins, and Richard Pervo, 3–19. Groningen: Barkuis, 2012.

Fagan, Garrett G. *The Lure of the Arena: Social Psychology and the Crowd at the Roman Games*. Cambridge: Cambridge University Press, 2011.

Finkelpearl, Ellen D. "Gender in the Ancient Novel." In *A Companion to the Ancient Novel*, edited by Edmund P. Cueva and Shannon N. Byrne, 455–72. West Sussex, UK: Wiley Blackwell, 2014.

Fidel, Kondwani. "The Dangerous Spectacle of Racist Violence Viral Videos." *Salon*. September 21, 2020. https://www.salon.com/2020/09/21/the-dangerous-spectacle-of-racist-violence-viral-videos-who-are-those-images-for.

Glancy, Jennifer A. "Protocols of Masculinity in the Pastoral Epistles." In *New Testament Masculinities*, edited by Stephen D. Moore and Janice Capel Anderson, 235–64. Semeia 45. Atlanta: Society of Biblical Literature, 2004.

———. *Slavery as a Moral Problem: In the Early Church and Today*. Facets. Minneapolis: Fortress Press, 2011.

Gleason, Maud. "The Semiotics of Gender: Physiognomy and Self-fashioning in the Second Century CE." In *Before Sexuality: The Construction of Erotic Experience in the Ancient Greek World*, edited by David Halperin, John Winkler, and Froma Zeitlin, 389–415. Princeton: Princeton University Press, 1990.

Global Americans. *Femicide and International Women's Rights: An Epidemic of Violence in Latin America*. 2017. https://theglobalamericans.org/reports/femicide-international-womens-rights.

Good, Deirdre J. "Early Extracanonical Writings." In *Women's Bible Commentary: Expanded Edition with Apocrypha*, edited by Carol Newsome and Sharon Ringe, 475–81. Louisville: Westminster John Knox, 1998.

Grant, Robert. "The Description of Paul in the Acts of Paul and Thecla." *Vigiliae Christianae* 36 (1982): 1–4.

Graverini, Lucia. "From the Epic to the Novelistic Hero: Some Patterns of a Metamorphosis." In *A Companion to the Ancient Novel*, edited by Edmund P. Cueva and Shannon N. Byrne, 288–99. West Sussex, UK: Wiley Blackwell, 2014.

Hanson, K. C. and Douglas E. Oakman. *Palestine in the Time of Jesus: Social Structures and Social Conflicts*. 2nd ed. Minneapolis: Fortress Press, 2008.

Hayes, Diana. *Forged in A Fiery Furnace: African American Spirituality*. Maryknoll, NY: Orbis Books, 2012.

Heine, Ronald. *The Montanist Oracles and Testimonia*. Patristic Monograph Series 14. Macon, GA: Mercer University Press, 1989.

Hilhorst, A. "Tertullian on the Acts of Paul." In *The Apocryphal Acts of Paul*, edited by Jan Bremmer, 150–63. Kampen, Netherlands: Kok Pharos, 1996.

Holmes, Brooke. *Gender: Antiquity and its Legacy*. Oxford: Oxford University Press, 2012.

———. "Marked Bodies: Gender, Race, Class, Age, Disability, and Disease." In *A Cultural History of the Human Body in Antiquity*, edited by Daniel Garrison, 159–83. Vol. 6 of *A Cultural History of the Human Body*, edited by Linda Kalof and William F. Bynum. Oxford: Berg Publishers, 2012.

Honey, Linda Ann. "Thekla: Text and Context with a First English Translation of the Miracles." PhD thesis, University of Calgary, 2011.

Horn, Cornelia. "Suffering Children, Parental Authority and the Quest for Liberation? A Tale of Three Girls in the *Acts of Paul (and Thecla)*, the *Act(s) of Peter*, the *Acts of Nerseus and Achilleus*, and the *Epistle of Pseudo-Titus*." In *A Feminist Companion to the New Testament Apocrypha*, edited by Amy-Jill Levine with Maria Mayo Robbins, 118–45. Feminist Companion to the New Testament and Early Christian Writings 11. Cleveland: The Pilgrim Press, 2006.

Hultin, Jeremy. "A New Web for Arachne and a New Veil for the Temple. Women and Weaving from Athena to the Virgin Mary." In *Women and Gender in Ancient Religions*, edited by Stephen P. Ahearne-Kroll, Paul A. Holloway, and James A. Kelhoffer, 209–23. Wissenschaftliche Untersuchungen zum Neuen Testament 263. Tübingen: Mohr Siebeck, 2010.

Hylen, Susan. *A Modest Apostle: Thecla and the History of Women in the Early Church*. Oxford: Oxford University Press, 2015.

Jackson, Melissa. "Lot's Daughters and Tamar as Tricksters and the Patriarchal Narratives as Feminist Theology." *Journal for the Study of the Old Testament* 26, no. 4 (2002): 29–46.

Jennings, Willie James. *The Christian Imagination: Theology and the Origins of Race*. New Haven, CT: Yale University Press, 2010.

———. *After Whiteness: An Education in Belonging*. Theological Education Between the Times. Grand Rapids, MI: Eerdmans, 2020.

Jensen, Anne. *Thekla—die Apostelin. Ein apokrypher Text neu entdeckt.* Kaiser-Taschenbücher 172. München: Gütersloh, 1999.

John, Renate. "Women in the Ancient Novel." In *The Novel in the Ancient World*, edited by Gareth Schmeling, 151–207. Leiden: Brill, 1996.

Johnson, Luke Timothy. *Among the Gentiles: Greco-Roman Religion and Christianity.* New Haven, CT: Yale University Press, 2009.

———. *The First and Second Letters to Timothy: A New Translation with Introduction and Commentary.* New York: Doubleday, 2001.

Johnson, Scott Fitzgerald. *The Life and Miracles of Thekla: A Literary Study.* Hellenic Studies Series 13. Washington, DC: Center for Hellenic Studies, 2006.

Johnson, Tiffany. "A Salute to Three Heroines of George Floyd Square." *Minnesota Spokesman Recorder.* April 7, 2021. https://spokesman-recorder.com/2021/05/23/a-salute-to-three-heroines-of-george-floyd-square.

Joubert, Stephan J. "Managing the Household: Paul as *Paterfamilias* of the Christian Household group in Corinth." In *Modelling Early Christianity: Social-Scientific Studies of the New Testament in its Context*, edited by Philip Esler, 213–23. London: Routledge, 1995.

Kee, Howard Clark. *Miracle in the Early Christian World: A Study in Sociohistorical Method.* New Haven, CT: Yale University Press, 1983.

Klauck, Hans-Josef. *The Apocryphal Acts of the Apostles: An Introduction.* Waco: Baylor University Press, 2008.

Kraemer, Ross Shepard. *Unreliable Witnesses: Religion, Gender and History in the Greco-Roman Mediterranean World.* Oxford: Oxford University Press, 2011.

Kraemer, Ross Shepard, and Mary Rose D'Angelo. *Women and Christian Origins.* Oxford: Oxford University Press, 1999.

Konstan, David. "Acts of Love: A Narrative Pattern in the Apocryphal Acts." *Journal of Early Christian Studies* 6, no. 1 (1998): 15–36.

Lampe, Peter. "Paul, Patrons, and Clients." In *Paul in the Greco-Roman World: A Handbook*, edited by J. Paul Sampley, 488–523. Harrisburg, PA: Trinity Press International, 2003.

Lefkowitz, Mary R. and Maureen B. Fant. *Women's Life in Greece and Rome: A Source Book in Translation.* 3rd ed. Baltimore: Johns Hopkins University Press, 2005.

Lemos, T. M. *Marriage Gifts and Social Change in Ancient Palestine: 1200 BCE to 200 CE.* Cambridge, UK: Cambridge University Press, 2010.

Lieu, Judith, M. "The 'Attraction of Women' in/to Early Judaism and Christianity: Gender and the Politics of Conversion." *Journal for the Study of the New Testament* 21, no. 72 (1998): 5–22.

Lipsett, Diane. *Desiring Conversion: Hermas, Thecla, Aseneth.* Oxford: Oxford University, 2011.

López Barja de Quiroga, Pedro. "Patronage and Slavery in the Roman World: The Circle of Power." In *The Oxford Handbook of Greek and Roman Slaveries*, edited by Stephen Hodkinson, Marc Kleijwegt, and Kostas Vlassopolous. Oxford: Oxford University Press, 2016.

MacDonald, Dennis R. *The Legend and the Apostle: The Battle for Paul in Story and Canon.* Philadelphia: Westminster, 1983.

MacDonald, Margaret Y. "Early Christian Women Married to Unbelievers." In *A Feminist Companion to the Deutero-Pauline Epistles*, edited by Amy-Jill Levine with Marianne Blickenstaff, 14–28. Cleveland: The Pilgrim Press, 2003.

———. *Early Christian Women and Pagan Opinion: The Power of the Hysterical Woman.* Cambridge, UK: Cambridge University Press, 1996.

Malherbe, Abraham. "A Physical Description of Paul." *Harvard Theological Review* 79, no. 1–3 (1986): 170–75.

Malina, Bruce J., and Jerome Neyrey. *Portraits of Paul: An Archaeology of Ancient Personality.* Louisville: Westminster John Knox, 1996.

Malina, Bruce J., and Richard L. Rorbaugh. *Social-Science Commentary on the Synoptic Gospels.* 2nd ed. Minneapolis: Fortress Press, 2003.

Marguerat, Daniel. "The *Acts of Paul* and the Canonical Acts: A Phenomenon of Rereading." Translated by Ken McKinney. *Semeia* 80 (1997): 169–83.

Marshall, Emily Zobel. "Anansi, Eshu, and Legba: Slave Resistance and the West African Trickster." In *Bonded Labour in the Cultural Contact Zone: Transdisciplinary Perspectives on Slavery and Its Discourses*, edited by Raphael Hörmann and Gesa Mackenthun, 171–92. Cultural Encounters and the Discourses of Scholarship 2. Münster: Waxmann, 2010.

———. "'Nothing but Pleasant Memories of the Discipline of Slavery': The Trickster and the Dynamics of Racial Representation." In *Marvels and Tales* 32, no. 1 (2018): 59–75.

Martin, Clarice J. "1–2 Timothy and Titus (The Pastoral Epistles)." In *True to Our Native Land: An African American New Testament Commentary*, edited by Brian Blount, 409–36. Minneapolis: Fortress Press, 2007.

Massingale, Bryan. *Racial Justice and the Catholic Church*. Maryknoll, NY: Orbis Books, 2010.

Matyszak, Philip. *24 Hours in Ancient Rome: A Day in the Life of People who Lived There*. London: Michael O'Mara, 2018.

McClure, Laura. *Spoken Like a Woman: Speech and Gender in Athenian Drama*. Princeton: Princeton University Press, 2009.

McGinn, Sheila. "The Acts of Thecla." In *Searching the Scriptures: A Feminist Commentary*, edited by Elisabeth Schüssler Fiorenza with the assistance of Ann Brock and Shelly Matthews, 800–828. New York: Crossroad, 1994.

McGinn, Thomas. *Prostitution, Sexuality, and the Law in Ancient Rome*. Oxford: Oxford University Press: 1998.

McLarty, J. D. *Thecla's Devotion: Narrative, Emotion and Identity in the Acts of Paul and Thecla*. Cambridge, UK: James Clarke & Co, 2018.

Millar, Fergus. "Condemnation to Hard Labour in the Roman Empire, from the Julio-Claudians to Constantine." *Papers of the British School at Rome* 52 (1984): 124–47.

Misset-van de Weg, Magda. "Answers to the Plight of an Ascetic Woman Named Thecla." In *A Feminist Companion to the New Testament Apocrypha*, edited by Amy-Jill Levine with Maria Mayo Robbins, 146–62. Cleveland: The Pilgrim Press, 2006.

———. "A Wealthy Woman named Tryphaena." In *The Apocryphal Acts of Paul and Thecla*, edited by Jan Bremmer, 16–35. Kampen, Netherlands: Kok Pharos, 1996.

Morales, Helen. *Antigone Rising: The Subversive Power of the Ancient Myths*. New York: Bold Type Books, 2020.

———. "The History of Sexuality." In *The Cambridge Companion to the Greek and Roman Novel*, edited by Tim Whitmarsh, 39–55. Cambridge, UK: Cambridge University Press, 2008.

Mitchell, Stephen. "An Epigraphic Probe into the Origins of Montanism." In *Roman Phrygia: Culture and Society*, edited by Peter Thonemann, 168–97. Cambridge, UK: Cambridge University Press, 2013.

Morgensen, Scott L. "White Settlers and Indigenous Solidarity: Confronting White Supremacy, Answering Decolonial Alliances." *Decolonization:*

Indigeneity, Education, and Society (blog). May 26, 2014. https://decolonization.wordpress.com/2014/05/26/white-settlers-and-indigenous-solidarity-confronting-white-supremacy-answering-decolonial-alliances/.

Moxnes, Halvor, ed. *Constructing Early Christian Families.* London: Routledge, 1997.

Nauerth, Claudia, and Rüdiger Warns. *Thekla, Ihre Bilder in der frühchristliche Kunst.* Wiesbaden, Germany: Harrassowitz, 1981.

Neyrey, Jerome. *Render to God: New Testament Understandings of the Divine.* Minneapolis: Fortress Press, 2004.

Niditch, Susan. *Underdogs and Tricksters: A Prelude to Biblical Folklore.* New Voices in Biblical Studies. San Francisco: Harper and Row, 1987.

O'Day, Gail R. "Gospel of John." In *Women's Bible Commentary,* edited by Carol Newsom, Sharon H. Ringe, and Jacqueline E. Lapsley, 529–30. 3rd ed. Louisville: Westminster John Knox, 2012.

Osiek, Carolyn, and Margaret MacDonald with Janet Tulloch. *A Woman's Place: House Churches in Earliest Christianity.* Minneapolis: Fortress, 2006.

Penn, Michael L., and Rahel Nardos. *Overcoming Violence against Women and Girls: The International Campaign to Eradicate a Worldwide Problem.* Lanham, MD: Rowman & Littlefield, 2003.

Perkins, Judith, "Space, Place and Voice in the Acts of the Martyrs and the Greek Romance." In *Mimesis and Intertextuality in Antiquity and Christianity,* edited by Dennis MacDonald, 117–37. Harrisburg, PA: Trinity Press International, 2001.

———. *The Suffering Self: Pain and Narrative Representation in the Early Christian Era.* London: Routledge, 1995.

———. "This World or Another? The Intertextuality of the Greek Romances, the Apocryphal Acts and Apuleius' Metamorphoses." *Semeia* 80 (1997): 247–60.

———. "Pastoral Epistles." In *Eerdmans Commentary on the Bible,* edited by James D. G. Dunn and John W. Rogerson, 1428–46. Grand Rapids, MI: Eerdmans, 2003.

Pervo, Richard I. *The Acts of Paul. A New Translation with Introduction and Commentary.* Eugene, OR: Cascade, 2014.

———. "Early Christian Fiction." In *Greek Fiction: The Greek Novel in Context,* edited by J. R. Morgan and R. Stoneman, 239–54. London: Routledge, 1994.

———. "The Hospitality of Onesiphorus: Missionary Styles and Support in the Acts of Paul." In *The Rise and Expansion of Christianity in the First Three Centuries of the Common Era*, edited by Clare K. Rothschild and Jens Schroter, 341–51. Tübingen: Mohr Siebeck, 2013.

———. *The Making of Paul: Constructions of the Apostle in Early Christianity.* Minneapolis: Fortress Press, 2010.

Pesthy, Monika. "Thekla among the Fathers of the Church." In *The Apocryphal Acts of Paul and Thecla*, edited by Jan Bremmer, 164–78. Kampen, Netherlands: Kok Pharos, 1996.

Peters, Edward M. "Prison before the Prison: The Ancient and Medieval Worlds." In *The Oxford History of the Prison: The Practice of Punishment in Western Society*, edited by Norval Morris and David J. Rothman, 3–43. Oxford: Oxford University Press, 1995.

Pfeil, Margaret. "A Spirituality of White Nonviolent Resistance to the Reality of Hyperincarceration." In *The Scandal of White Complicity in US Hyper-Incarceration: A Nonviolent Spirituality of White Resistance*, 143–66. London: Palgrave MacMillan, 2013.

Phillips, Thomas E. *Paul, His Letters, and Acts.* Grand Rapids, MI: Baker Academic, 2009.

Pilgrim, Walter E. *Uneasy Neighbors: Church and State in the New Testament.* Minneapolis: Fortress Press, 1999.

Plevnik, Joseph. "Honor/Shame." In *Handbook of Biblical Social Values*, edited by John J. Pilch and Bruce J. Malina, 106–15. 3rd ed. Eugene, OR: Wipf and Stock, 2013.

Porter, Stanley E. "What Does it Mean to be 'Saved by Childbirth?' (1 Tim 2:15)." *Journal for the Study of the New Testament* 49 (1993): 87–102.

Potter, David. "Martyrdom as Spectacle." In *Theater and Society in the Classical World*, edited by Ruth Scodel, 53–88. Ann Arbor: University of Michigan Press, 1993.

Price, S. R. F. *Rituals and Power: The Roman Imperial Cult in Asia Minor.* Cambridge, UK: Cambridge University Press, 1984.

Radermacher, Ludwig. *Hippolytos und Thekla: Studien zur Geschichte von Legende und Kultus.* Sitzungsberichte Akademie der Wissenschaften in Wien, Philosophisch-Historische Klasse 182, no. 3. Vienna: Hölder, 1916.

Ralph, Laurence. *The Torture Letters: Reckoning with Police Violence.* Chicago: University of Chicago Press, 2020.

Richardson, Alyssa V. *Bearing Witness While Black: African Americans, Smartphones, and the New Protest #Journalism*. Oxford: Oxford University Press, 2020.

Robinson, Elaine A. *Race and Theology*. Horizons in Theology. Nashville: Abingdon, 2012.

Robinson, O. F. *Penal Practice and Penal Policy in Ancient Rome*. London: Routledge, 2007.

Rohrbaugh, Richard L. *The New Testament in Cross-Cultural Perspective*. Matrix: The Bible in Mediterranean Context. Eugene, OR: Cascade Books, 2006.

Rordorf, Willy. "In welchem Verhältnis stehen die apokryphen Paulusakten zur kanonischen Apostelgeschichte und zu den Pastoralbriefen?" In *Text and Testimony: Essays on New Testament and Apocryphal Literature in Honour of A.F.J. Klijn*, edited by T. Baarda, A. Hilhorst, G. P. Luttikhuizen and A. S. van der Woude, 225–41. Kampen, Netherlands: Kok Pharos, 1988.

———. "La Prière de sainte Thècle pour une dèfunte païenne et son importance oecuménique." In *Liturgie, foi et vie des premiers chrétiens*, 445–55. Études patristiques, Theologie historique 75. Paris: Beauchesne, 1986.

———. "Tradition and Composition in the Acts of Thecla: The State of the Question." *Semeia* 38 (1986): 43–52.

Roy, Kalpana. *Encyclopedia of Violence Against Women and Dowry Death in India*. New Delhi: Anmol Publications, 1999.

Schneider, Horst. "Thekla und die Robben." *Vigiliae Christianae* 55, no. 1 (2001): 45–57.

Schneiders, Sandra M. *Women and the Word: The Gender of God in the New Testament and the Spirituality of Women*. 1986 Madeleva Lecture in Spirituality. Mahwah, NJ: Paulist Press, 1986.

Schüssler Fiorenza, Elisabeth. *In Memory of Her: A Feminist Theological Reconstruction of Christian Origins*. New York: Crossroad Publishing, 1983.

———. "Word, Spirit and Power: Women in Early Christian Communities." In *Women of Spirit: Female Leadership in the Jewish and Christian Traditions*, edited by Rosemary Ruether and Eleanor McLaughlin, 29–70. New York: Simon and Schuster, 1979.

Segal, Alan. *Life After Death: A History of the Afterlife in Western Religion*. New York: Random House, 2004.

Smith, Abraham. "Paul and African American Biblical Interpretation." In *True to Our Native Land: An African American New Testament Commentary*, edited by Brian K. Blount, Cain Hope Felder, Clarice J. Martin, and Emerson B. Powery, 31–38. Minneapolis: Fortress Press, 2007.

Smith, Mitzi J. "Slavery in the Early Church." In *True to Our Native Land: An African American New Testament Commentary*, edited by Brian K. Blount, Cain Hope Felder, Clarice J. Martin, and Emerson B. Powery, 11–19. Minneapolis: Fortress Press, 2007.

Smith, Mitzi, and Yung Suk Kim. *Toward Decentering the New Testament: A Reintroduction*. Eugene, OR: Cascade, 2018.

Snyder, Glenn E. *Acts of Paul: The Formation of a Pauline Corpus*. Tübingen: Mohr Siebeck, 2013.

Soards, Marion L. *The Apostle Paul: An Introduction to His Writings and Teachings*. Mahwah, NJ: Paulist Press, 1987.

Solevåg, Anna. *Birthing Salvation: Gender and Class in Early Christian Childbearing Discourse*. Leiden: Koninklijke Brill NV, 2013.

Spittler, Janet E. *Animals in the Apocryphal Acts of the Apostles*. Wissenschaftliche Untersuchungen zum Neuen Testament 263. Tübingen: Mohr Siebeck, 2008.

St. Clair, Raquel. "Womanist Biblical Interpretation." In *True to Our Native Land: An African American New Testament Commentary*, edited by Brian K. Blount, Cain Hope Felder, Clarice Jannette Martin, and Emerson B. Powery, 54–62. Minneapolis: Fortress Press, 2007.

Streete, Gail. *Redeemed Bodies: Women Martyrs in Early Christianity*. Louisville: Westminster John Knox, 2009.

Stowers, Stanley. "Paul and Self-Mastery." In *Paul in the Greco-Roman World: A Handbook*, edited by J. Paul Sampley, 270–300. Harrisburg, PA: Trinity Press International, 2003.

Tabbernee, William. *Montanist Inscriptions and Testimonia: Epigraphic Sources Illustrating the History of Montanism*. Patristic Monograph Series 16. Macon, GA: Mercer University Press, 1997.

Thomas, Christine. "The Scriptures and the New Prophecy: Montanism as Exegetical Crisis." In *Early Christian Voices: In Texts, Traditions, and Symbols*, edited by David Warren, Ann Graham Brock, and David Pao, 155–65. Leiden: Brill, 2002.

———. "Stories Without Texts and Without Authors: The Problem of Fluidity in Ancient Novelistic Texts and Early Christian Literature." In *New Perspectives on Ancient Fiction and the New Testament*, edited by Ronald F. Hock, J. Bradley Chance, and Judith Perkins, 273–91. Atlanta: Scholars Press, 1998.

Thurman, Howard. *Jesus and the Disinherited*. Boston: Beacon, 1949.

Thurston, Bonnie. "1 Timothy 5:3–16 and the Leadership of Women in the Early Church." In *A Feminist Companion to the Deutero-Pauline Epistles*, edited by Amy-Jill Levine with Marianne Blickenstaff, 159–74. Cleveland: The Pilgrim Press, 2003.

Tinker, George. *American Indian Liberation: A Theology of Sovereignty*. Maryknoll, NY: Orbis Books, 2008.

Tolbert, Mary Ann. "Mark." In *Women's Bible Commentary: Expanded Edition with Apocrypha*, edited by Carol Newsom and Sharon Ringe, 350–62. Louisville: Westminster John Knox, 1998.

Trevett, Christine. *Montanism, Gender, Authority and the New Prophecy*. Cambridge, UK: Cambridge University Press, 1996.

Trible, Phyllis. *God and the Rhetoric of Sexuality*. Minneapolis: Fortress Press, 1978.

Trumbower, Jeffery. *Rescue for the Dead: The Posthumous Salvation of Non-Christians in Early Christianity*. Oxford: Oxford University Press, 2001.

Vander Stichele, Caroline and Todd Penner. *Contextualizing Gender in Early Christian Discourse*. London: T&T Clark, 2009.

Vorster, J. N. "Construction of Culture through the Construction of Person: the Acts of Thecla as an Example." In *A Feminist Companion to the New Testament Apocrypha*, edited by Amy-Jill Levine with Maria Mayo Robbins, 98–117. Cleveland: The Pilgrim Press, 2006.

Waziyatawin. *What Does Justice Look Like? The Struggle for Liberation in Dakota Homeland*. St. Paul, MN: Living Justice Press, 2008.

Weaver, Paul. *Familia Caesaris: A Social Study of the Emperor's Freedmen and Slaves*. Cambridge, UK: Cambridge University Press, 1972.

Wehn, Beate. "'Blessed are the Bodies of Those Who are Virgins': Reflections on the Image of Paul in the Acts of Thecla." *Journal for the Study of the New Testament* 79 (2000): 149–64.

———. "'Ich bin Sklavin des lebendigen Gottes!' Die Apostolin Thekla: Von Grenzüber-schreitungen und ihren Folgen." In *GrenzgängerInnen:*

Unterwegs zu einer anderen biblischen Theologie: Ein feministisch-theologisches Lesebuch, edited by Claudia Janssen, Ute Ochtendung, and Beate Wehn, 35–48. Mainz: Matthias-Grünewald-Verlag, 1999.

Also available in English translation: "'I am a Handmaid of the Living God!' The Apostle Thecla and the Consequences of Transgression." In *Transgressors: Toward a Feminist Biblical Theology*. Edited by Claudia Janssen, Ute Ochtendung, and Beate Wehn. Translated by Linda M. Maloney, 19–30. Collegeville, MN: The Liturgical Press, 2002.

Wheatley, Alan. *Patronage in Early Christianity: Its Use and Transformation from Jesus to Paul of Samosata*. Princeton: Princeton University Press, 2011.

White, L. Michael. "Paul and *Pater Familias*." In *Paul in the Greco-Roman World: A Handbook*, edited by J. Paul Sampley, 457–87. Harrisburg, PA: Trinity Press International, 2003.

Whitmarsh, Tim. *Dirty Love: The Genealogy of the Ancient Greek Novel*. Oxford: Oxford University Press, 2018.

Zamfir, Korinna. "The Topos of Female Hiddenness. A Contextual Reading of 1 Tim 2,9–15." *Ephemerides Theologicae Lovanienses* 88, no. 4 (2012): 475–87.

———. "Shipwrecked, Enemies and Deserters? The Opponents and their Function in the Pastoral Epistles and the Acts of Paul and Thecla." In *Gegenspieler*, edited by Michael Tilly and Ulrich Mell, 281–310. Tübingen: Mohr Siebeck, 2019.

Zanetto, Giuseppe. "Greek Novel and Greek Archaic Literature." In *A Companion to the Ancient Novel*, edited by Edmund P. Cueva and Shannon N. Byrne, 400–410. West Sussex, UK: Wiley Blackwell, 2014.

Index of Subjects

179

Index of Authors

182

Index of Ancient Sources